D0411632

Quality in Public Services

Public Policy and Management

Series Editor: Professor R.A.W. Rhodes, Department of Politics, University of York.

The effectiveness of public policies is a matter of public concern and the efficiency with which policies are put into practice is a continuing problem for governments of all political persuasions. This series contributes to these debates by publishing informed, in-depth and contemporary analyses of public administration, public policy and public management.

The intention is to go beyond the usual textbook approach to the analysis of public policy and management and to encourage authors to move debate about their issue forward. In this sense, each book both describes current thinking and research, and explores future policy directions. Accessibility is a key feature and, as a result, the series will appeal to academics and their students as well as to the informed practitioner.

Current Titles Include:

Whose Utility? The Social Impact of Public Utility Privatization and Regulation in Britain
John Ernst

Quality in Public Services: Managers' Choices
Lucy Gaster

Transforming Central Government: The Next Steps Initiative
Patricia Greer

Implementing Thatcherite Policies: Audit of an Era
David Marsh and R.A.W. Rhodes (eds)

British Aid and International Trade
O. Morrissey, B. Smith and E. Horesh

Markets and Managers: New Issues in the Delivery of Welfare
Peter Taylor-Gooby and Robyn Lawson (eds)

Social Care in a Mixed Economy
Gerald Wistow, Martin Knapp, Brian Hardy and Caroline Allen

New Managerialism: Administrative Reform in Whitehall and Canberra
Spencer Zifcak

Quality in Public Services

Managers' Choices

Lucy Gaster

Open University Press
Buckingham · Philadelphia

For Nick

Open University Press
Celtic Court
22 Ballmoor
Buckingham
MK18 1XW

and
1900 Frost Road, Suite 101
Bristol, PA 19007, USA

First Published 1995

A catalogue record of this book is available from the British Library

ISBN   0 335 19160 6 (pbk)   0 335 19349 8 (hbk)

Library of Congress Cataloging-in-Publication Data
Gaster, Lucy, 1940–
     Quality in public services : managers' choices / Lucy Gaster.
        p.   cm. – (Public policy and management)
     Includes bibliographical references and index.
     ISBN 0-335-19349-8 — ISBN 0-335-19160-6 (pbk.)
     1. Public administration – Great Britain.   2. Municipal services –
     Great Britain – Management.   I. Title.   II. Services.
     JN425.G375 1994
     363'.068–dc20   94-25735
                                                                          CIP

Typeset by Dorwyn Ltd, Rowlands Castle, Hants
Printed in Great Britain by Biddles Ltd, Guildford and King's Lynn

Contents

Preface

For years I had been sitting meekly in dreary hospital corridors; I had been trying not to antagonize the dustmen by asking them to pick up their dropped rubbish; I had been tripping over uneven paving stones; and I had, when elderly relatives could no longer cope for themselves, tried to find my way through the bureaucratic maze to get help from the social services. This all seemed 'normal', if very frustrating. I was not, however, in the power of any public authority – was not a council tenant or a social service client, I had no major illnesses and I had a job. I could cope.

In 1977, the part of inner London where I had been living for fifteen years was declared a 'Housing Action Area'. Having recently become involved in a local residents' group and been appointed a school governor, I found myself on the Council joint subcommittee overseeing the process (owner-occupiers and private tenants had to elect separate representatives). Here was a new facet of public services, imposed in a rule-bound, insensitive and even threatening way. (How would you feel if an environmental health officer – a what? – jumped on your floor, prodded your walls and window-sills and produced long, jargon-ridden 'notices', stuck to the door if no-one was in?) The role of advocate, interpreter (after a rather rapid learning curve), mediator and networker became second nature. What was it, we asked ourselves, that made perfectly ordinary decent human beings turn into officious and defensive ogres when they put their local government hat on? Why did the councillors not stand up for local people? Why, when some officers were so helpful, were others inaccessible and unresponsive?

In 1982, when I jumped the fence and became a local government officer, it became possible to see from the 'inside' what was happening, though it was still difficult to understand why. But in the mid-1980s, when I became a neighbourhood officer in the newly decentralized London Borough of Islington, the need both to understand and to try to make changes became imperative. Decentralization was a policy that was to 'break down barriers', to make the Council more responsive to local people, even (cautiously) to involve local communities in decision-making. How was this to be done? A naïve belief in the idea that a new structure would automatically bring about the changes we hoped for soon gave way to the realization that it was far more complicated than that. Four years later, there had been a lot of 'learning from mistakes', but very little progress on developing tools and methods either to improve the services provided through the neighbourhood offices, or to monitor or measure their quality.

When I started to work seriously on the question of service quality – after I had left local government – there was still, at the end of the 1980s, very little material that seemed relevant to the problems and dilemmas that I as a public service manager had had to face. When I wrote *Quality at the front line* in 1989 (published by the School for Advanced Urban Studies in 1991), I felt I was treading in new territory, at least as far as local government was concerned.

Since then, 'quality' has come onto the public agenda in a big way. Some of the reasons for this may be questionable, but my starting point for this book is that it is valid, right and proper to see the improvement of public service quality as a high priority. What now concerns me is that the concept of quality is in danger of being distorted. The simplistic and missionary way it is often presented and introduced into public service organizations can easily alienate staff, without convincing either them or the public of the utility and practicability of the policy. This means that it is not durable and that other, newer issues will soon push it aside.

At the same time, there are many forces coming together to press 'quality' into a particular mould. This, paradoxically, is a mould that bears remarkable similarities to all that those who see quality as embodied in sensitive, flexible, fair and minimally bureaucratic services were trying to get away from. The pressure on individuals to conform and compete with each other places the emphasis on reaching achievable, generally quantitative targets, on procedure-based 'quality assurance' and on standardized 'fault-free' services.

My idea in writing this book has been to try, on the basis of my own experience and research, and using the ever-increasing literature on the subject, to question some assumptions and to analyse critically where the debate on quality is going.

Quality is not a neutral, technical affair, though it is often presented as such. Gurus – there are an awful lot of them in the quality field – tend to make statements of the 'just follow me and I shall lead you to salvation' type. We have many handbooks and guidance on 'how to' (and sometimes 'how not to'). They often focus on processes, looking at means but not ends. We seem to be short of assessments of quality that take a more dispassionate, even sceptical approach. It is this gap that I am ambitiously trying to fill.

The framework I use puts values at the centre. It also requires the active involvement of consumers, citizens and front-line staff, as well as a whole host of other 'interests'. Public services are owned by and responsible to the public, who need a say in what they consist of and how they are run. And service users (past, potential and present) are not 'customers' in the sense of being able to vote with their feet or their purse: they are often forced to receive services or are excluded from them through the decisions of others. They too need a say in the quality of services.

Some of the tensions and contradictions I identify in this book will be well known to managers, in all public services, not just local government. Taking an optimistic view, I think it is possible to consider quality rationally and systematically. Those responsible for or contributing to policies to improve quality should be better able to control their own destiny: they should be able to make choices for the benefit of their service users, their staff and for the public as a whole. If public services are to survive, choices about quality *must* be made.

Lucy Gaster
Birmingham

Acknowledgements

My ideas about quality in the public services have been evolving over quite a long period, as a community member, a local government officer and in the course of research about a whole range of different topics. I have had a lot of support from very many people, and have been very lucky. I should particularly like to thank Patricia Richards, who was a wonderful colleague in Islington, and Kieron Walsh, who in 1989 gave me some crucial footholds (is this the right metaphor?) when I was beginning to find my way round the then existing literature on quality. Students on the MSc course on Management Development and Social Responsibility at the School for Advanced Urban Studies were very patient and constructively critical when I was trying out my ideas and frameworks with them, as have been workers from many local government and voluntary sector organizations who came to the short courses on quality that we began to run at the School in 1990. Among many colleagues at SAUS with whom I have worked in the last four years, I should particularly like to thank Marilyn Taylor, Linda Martin and Cynthia Galliers.

Rachel and Peter Baird have been consistently supportive and interested while I was struggling with the writing in Birmingham, and Pat Lee and John Skelton at the Open University Press were wonderfully understanding.

My family probably never want to hear the word 'quality' again. Ah well, they will!

1

Introduction

The argument for reliable, sensitive and efficient services holds good however and by whom they are supplied. The history of public services, established over the last century in recognition of the need for 'public goods' to meet the needs of all members of society, and until recently supplied exclusively by 'the public sector', is that such an assumption cannot be taken for granted. Low quality services, generating and perpetuating low expectations, have too often been the experience – of both users and producers of those services. Dissatisfaction, frustration, but not much action was the result.

Now the situation is different. Quality in public services is recognized as the right of all citizens. The problem is that simplistic rhetoric and partial solutions may actually be undermining what quality is, or should be, about.

Public service workers may have an 'ideal conception' of their jobs (Lipsky 1980), but the pressures on them – too much demand, too little supply; unclear and ambiguous goals, isolation at the front line and low expectations of (often involuntary) service users – leads to the corner-cutting and low morale. Conscious and systematic efforts to develop and maintain high quality could restore self-confidence and pride in the job: staff will know what they are meant to be doing and will be supported to do it well; goodwill and support will be generated from users and public. Quality projects up and down the country show this is possible.

Many conditions need to be fulfilled before quality policies can be effective. Top-down, cookbook ideas will never have a lasting impact on those who have to carry them out – the front-line staff. Yet it is largely on the willingness, understanding and commitment of these staff that a quality policy will stand or fall.

What do we need to know about quality?

If ensuring quality was easy, everyone would have done it by now. So what are the basic ingredients of a discussion of quality? Where do we start?

The questions to which managers need answers are:

- How is quality defined?
- How is it measured?
- How is it put into practice?
- How is it maintained?
- Whose quality is it?

From these arise other questions, notably:

- What is the business we are in, what are we trying to do?
- How can all these issues be linked together?
- What choices do I have for how I (and my organization) go about it?

I shall look briefly at these issues before proposing a model for understanding and pursuing them more systematically.

Defining quality

There is no agreed definition of quality, yet it is this that anyone wanting to improve their service hankers for. It is one thing to define what you are trying to achieve, another to pin down the dimensions and characteristics that, together, constitute its quality. Some people take an all-inclusive view, some try to narrow it down (I am one of these) to those aspects of service that are not covered by other public management requirements, such as efficiency, equality or equity. The 'gurus' tend not to define quality at all, except in broad terms such as 'conformance to specification' or 'fitness for purpose'. Neither of these definitions takes the manager trying to improve the quality of her or his service a great deal further.

Systematic attention to detail, within a strategic framework of policies and values, is possibly the key to quality. So defining that detail is essential to any quality policy: it is a guide to deciding priorities in implementation, it gives a starting point for developing service standards, and it is the basis for monitoring and evaluation.

Measuring quality

One of the first questions that is often asked is: how do we know what is the quality of our work unless we can measure it? Measurement and monitoring are certainly an important part of the story. But there is a risk that this process becomes an end in itself. Concentration on developing measurable 'standards' may leave out the aspects of service that really matter to people: accurate responses, sensitive listening, discussion of options and so on. Measurements can be manipulated. And, unless there is a clear policy and values framework, how are the results to be interpreted: what is 'good', what is 'bad'?

Tempting though it is to 'do' quality by setting up inspection units, developing standards, counting transactions and publishing satisfaction surveys, none of this is meaningful without a broader context.

Strategic objectives

It became clear to me when I began to work on quality issues that starting with measurements was the wrong way round. What was it that was being measured? Had the service – and the nature of its quality – been defined? What was intended to be achieved? Were objectives known to and accepted by the staff responsible for putting them into practice?

Most people in most public services have for many years operated without clear objectives, and some of those services have been of high quality (surely?). Even if objectives are clearly defined, circumstances can change; other, possibly contradictory objectives emerge; those objectives that do exist are sometimes hard to translate into action. So it would be unwise to argue that clear objectives are a *sine qua non* of quality in action. However, it would be equally difficult to argue that consistency and a systematic approach to service quality could be developed without some idea of strategic objectives.

Values

Strategic objectives are derived from values, whether explicit (as in 'mission' or 'vision' statements) or hidden. The gap between stated values and those that in reality guide day-to-day activity may itself be wide, and, even in organizations that have (usually after a lot of effort) managed to define their values, it may be a struggle to maintain them when other values, particularly those associated with 'business systems', threaten to displace them.

Tensions may also exist between managerial and political values that profess to drive the organization, and professional values or personal values held by individuals. Yet, however difficult to articulate and disentangle, an understanding and recognition of values – not often discussed by the quality gurus, by the way – is essential to an understanding of public sector quality. Indeed, interpreting the now endless stream of charters and standards emerging from private businesses, utilities and banks in terms of their implied value base can be illuminating. What are the real values that inform their actions, by which you can assess how you and others in the community will be treated in practice? What is *their* quality?

Putting quality into practice

Much of the public debate on quality in the three or four years preceding the writing of this book has been dominated by discussions and assertions about quality systems – about quality control, quality assurance, total quality management and customer care. Central Government's emphasis on the Citizen's Charter (and its offspring) has reinforced this trend. Of course it is important to be able to think clearly about how to put concepts of quality into practice – otherwise they simply remain paper policies – but it is equally important to be clear what those concepts are, where they came from, why they were chosen. The danger that management practices are imported inappropriately and without due rationale makes them very vulnerable to opposition and resistance, to loss of credibility in the community and with service users, and ultimately, 'failure' of the policy itself. An implementation system has to grow logically and naturally from an analysis of where an organization is, where it wants to get to, and what factors already exist that can help or hinder the move from the first state to the second. This can only be done on the basis of a proper diagnosis, involving all those who will later be responsible for making it work.

Many organizations responsible for providing public services have been taking a hard look at their management and policy-making systems. While some have been developing cultures that tend to emphasize the role of the individual and the priority of 'winning' or 'surviving', others have been looking at themselves to see how best they can build on the experience, knowledge and skills of their staff, and how they can build an organizational infrastructure that encourages efficiency within an atmosphere of co-operation and public service orientation. They may well be at a 'take-off' point for implementing policies for quality. External quality systems may even be at odds with what they are trying to achieve. Searching questions need to be asked before hiring expensive consultants to help develop a system that may be irrelevant and, eventually, unsustainable.

Whose quality?

The last few paragraphs have tended to look at quality from a rather traditional, managerial point of view. A rounded perspective is essential when considering quality; otherwise quality has little meaning – for the consumer, for the citizen or for the employee. This makes it unlikely to succeed. One of the key ingredients for effective quality policies, endorsed by all the writers on the subject, is the need for commitment and understanding at all organizational levels. In the private sector, a 'customer orientation' is considered essential. In public services, I would argue that not only should there be a public service orientation among providers, but that citizens and consumers should also have an *active* role in improving quality.

It may be tempting to be totally consumerist – to take the view that the customer knows best. Even if this is true (and where does it leave the 'professionals'?) it does not require an intimate knowledge of market economics to know that the customer can only 'know best' if she or he has full knowledge of the product or service in question, and can back an informed choice with the power of the purse and with self-confidence. These conditions rarely hold in the market place, far less so in the realm of the public services, where choices are restricted through statute or resources and where services are often complex, technical and cannot be bought.

To base a policy for quality on the proposition that the customer knows best is therefore questionable. And even when consumers have enough knowledge and put it to use, other forces come into play. The interests of other 'customers', or of the community at large, expressed though policy and legislation, may over-ride the wishes of individual customers or consumers. Resources, too, restrict the service provider's power to meet needs and supply wants.

Nevertheless, the idea that consumers have a right to express their views and in some degree to determine policies about public services is compelling, if only for the very reasons spelt out above: they do not have the power of perfect knowledge, of choice, or of the purse. It is doubly important to build other ways of finding out what services consumers need and what they will accept.

Consulting with users, their families and carers is not enough. Many other people have an interest – past or future – in a service without having a direct link at a particular moment. Direct and institutional discrimination can exclude people altogether. A community perspective may be very different from and sometimes clash directly with that of individual consumers: dog nuisance in public parks is an issue that comes instantly to mind; planning applications is another.

The third group to which I wish to pay attention at this stage is front-line staff. It is sad but true that these are often the least valued staff of any organization, yet they are the part of the organization by which the rest is judged by the public and the outside world. They also have a detailed knowledge of the needs, wishes, likes and dislikes of their users and may well know far more about the local community than the policy-makers sitting in Town Halls, District Health Authority offices or Training and Enterprise Council headquarters situated in town centres, business parks and the like.

For any one service, there will be a range of interests who all feel they have a right or duty to become involved in the business of quality. There are others – elected councillors – who are perhaps wrongly excluded, on the grounds that quality is a management issue.

It is difficult to know how many different parties can realistically be engaged in what has to be a detailed and time-consuming business of quality. Maybe the extent of involvement of all the different interests – councillors, trades unions, community and voluntary groups, boards of management – in quality issues is as much a matter for them as for the organization. But opportunities need to be created and nurtured for that involvement to be effective.

A rational model for quality

Having looked at some of the main ingredients of a policy for quality – definitions, measurements, objectives, values, systems and interests – it is time to bring them together.

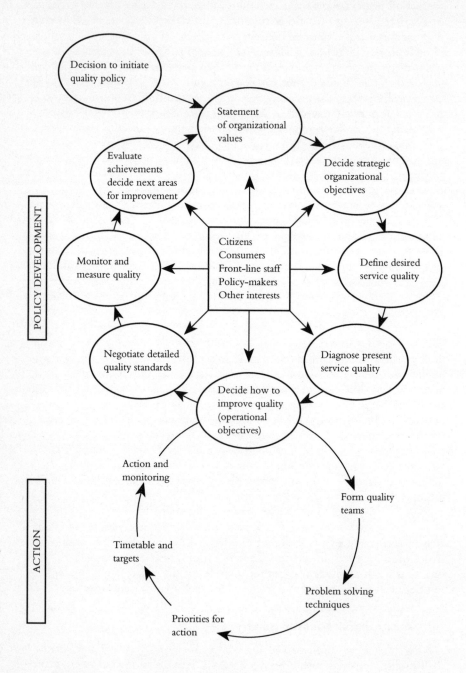

Figure 1.1   A model for service quality

So I want to put forward a model and use it as the framework for the rest of this book; partly as an aid to thinking – to see the connections between the different aspects of policies for quality – partly as an aid to action. It is a rational model, assuming the use of reasoning (the Latin '*ratio*' = 'reason'), in contrast to dependence on instinct and emotion. It links the different processes that make up a complete policy cycle in a logical order, and assumes that the next area of activity depends on the outcome of the previous one.

Such a model can be criticized, perfectly reasonably, on the grounds that rational policy implementation models provide an unsatisfactory explanation for how events take place in reality. As a prescriptive model, the rational approach also has weaknesses, especially on the grand scale of national policies. Too many extraneous factors intervene between concept and execution, and it is never possible to be sure that the policies were relevant and appropriate in the first place.

However, at the level of a single organization, even a large and complex one, such a model has considerable advantages for policy formation and implementation. The main advantages are:

- Relationships between different parts of the policy process are clarified.
- It is easy to see why particular activities, such as performance measurement, should not be tackled in isolation from values and objectives.
- A rational approach provides a weapon against *ad hoc*ery and fragmentation.

It would be foolish and impractical to claim that slippage does not take place between policy formation and the different levels of implementation within any one organization. External factors can change priorities, sometimes almost overnight, and throw the tidiest system into disarray. Both formal and informal discretion in day-to-day practice means that policy implementation can vary enormously (maybe too much) within a single organization.

However, it is worth noting that the more devolved the system for decision-making, allowing formal discretion as near the point of service delivery as possible, the more necessary a clear policy framework becomes. This is the 'tight–loose' model increasingly espoused by exponents of the 'new managerialism' (Hoggett 1991), as well as being the system advocated by some of the quality gurus, particularly Peters and Waterman (1982). It fits well, as will be seen, with ideas about public service quality: the tight–loose organizational structure is based on a policy implementation model very like the one I suggest here.

A scientific, rational policy underlies medical and engineering advances. Quality should not simply be seen as a modern version of alchemy. A (rational) model brings some order to the debate, and enables practitioners and the public to see the policy as a whole. From this, suitable areas of policy and action can be located for practical involvement or influence.

The main features of the model presented in Figure 1.1 are:

- It shows the relationship between values, strategic objectives and the processes of implementation, including the development of quality standards.

- It provides a basis for mapping different quality systems into the whole process: measurement systems would be in one place, quality assurance in another, while the development of standards can be separately identified.
- It therefore makes it easier to be clear about what each quality system or approach does *not* cover as well as what it does.
- Although it is not intended to make it seem as if the same ground will be gone over again and again, it does demonstrate the continuous nature of the process, a learning cycle.
- Last but not least, it shows how the great range of people with an 'interest' or 'stake' in the proceedings could or should become involved at each of the different points round the circle.

Structure of the book

Following from the model just introduced, the rest of this book is structured as follows.

To set the scene, I shall complete this chapter with a discussion of values and objectives. This provides a context for the next two chapters, where we look at definitions: whose they are and where they come from. It is at this point, as well as at several other moments, that the distinction will need to be made between the origins of much of the debate, rooted as they are in private sector manufacturing, and the use of the concept of quality in public services.

The next stage is to consider the practical question of *how* quality is achieved. No magic answers are suggested, but some of the ingredients that may contribute to or detract from a potentially successful quality policy will be examined. The question of organizational structures, cultures and style are all important, as are systems, procedures and the availability of problem-solving techniques. At the same time, a critical look will be taken at quality control, quality assurance, total quality management, British Standard (BS) 5750, customer care and a whole array of 'recipes' for improving and maintaining service quality.

Following on from this, the particular issue of standards and charters needs to be addressed. Are standards a constraint on the flexibility and sensitivity required for many personal services? They may provide a basis for redress and fairness but are they in fact enforceable? How are they put together, and what happens if circumstances change?

Although measuring quality is not easy, especially for those addicted to the use of quantitative data, it is an integral part of any quality policy. So Chapter 7 will look at ideas and experience concerning measurement, including the distorting effects of performance measures, the role of the front line staff in both monitoring and evaluation, and how the public can and should be involved in the process.

The quality debate is full of tensions and contradictions. For public services, these are intensified by the pressures of business cultures, enforced competition and division between those responsible for the services (as purchasers or enablers) and those providing them.

In the final chapter, then, I think about the main components of a policy for public service quality and explore how far public sector managers can in reality pursue the development of high quality in their services. The question is simple: how can managers deal with all the competing demands on their energies and resources, and where does quality come in the hierarchy of policy priorities? The answer is, of course, more complicated. Even so, I conclude that improving the quality of services to the public – whoever actually delivers them – is both realistic and important, and crucial to their survival.

Values in quality

The question of values covers not only how quality is defined in an organization, but how it is interpreted and, most important of all, how it is implemented. This is demonstrated through, for example, how staff and consumers are consulted, who gets listened to, the style of leadership and other cultural factors. So values are the starting point for the whole quality debate.

Values of, say, equality and empowerment, or of interventionism, will have very different effects on how quality is defined and implemented than, for example, economy, profits and market share. An organization whose philosophy is to commission rather than directly to provide services will be different again. In each case, different priorities and trade-offs will be chosen, different people and groups will be involved in design, implementation and evaluation of a high quality service. It is important to recognize this, and to be able to test policies that purport to be 'quality' policies against their underlying values, at political, managerial or local team levels. It is also important to check what is said against what is actually done. There may be a (big) difference between the espoused values and those in use. At the same time, within a single organization different perspectives and values will exist. Discovering the dominant set of values can be difficult if they are not stated explicitly.

Quality initiatives are difficult to sustain. If they fail, it may be because they have not become embedded within the culture. They are often perceived as an 'add-on' process, particularly when they are imposed from above as the latest management idea. When quality is seen as the 'flavour of the month', unconnected with the basic organizational purpose and priorities and irrelevant to individuals' practice – just another thing to 'do' and get out of the way – it runs the highest risk of being discredited. If quality arises naturally from organizational values, this could be a way of keeping the policy together, of providing the 'glue'.

To read some of the gurus, it would be easy to suppose that quality is a value-free concept, aiming to achieve something as apparently scientific and neutral as statistical control, conformance to specification, non-variation, uniformity, standardization (Crosby 1986; Deming 1986). The implication is that you only need to get your systems right – which generally includes staff training and awareness – and you are well away.

Certainly, much of the discussion of quality in the early 1990s seems to have revolved around the notion that the mere fact of installing a quality system – quality assurance, for example, with BS 5750 as a specific variant – would produce a quality end-result. Or that the declaration of some service 'standard' will in itself lead to the production of a high quality service. Yet underlying all these activities are unspoken value systems. Acknowledging what they are is a first step towards defining quality itself.

How are value systems expressed?

Some large private sector firms, including some which have long given a high profile to high quality (Marks and Spencer and Sainsburys are obvious British examples in the service sector) profess a social or philanthropic role, often expressed through charitable and research foundations. However, it is unclear how or whether such values are translated into the production side of the enterprise. The bottom line of profits (however defined) and market share are inherently the driving force for quality improvements. It was the Japanese post-war drive to compete in world markets that led the American writers Dr W. Edwards Deming and Dr Joseph Juran to be invited to Japan in the early 1950s to develop their quality systems in that country. The success of the Japanese competition led later gurus, such as Crosby and Peters and Waterman, to look at how to improve quality and 'excellence' in the United States.

Interestingly, Peters and Waterman (1982 Chapter 9) do put a lot of emphasis on clear value systems. They suggest the importance not only of clear and constant communication of the values to the rest of the organization but also of the efficacy of carrying out this communication in person – by senior managers and, often, by a charismatic leader. Their 'excellent' firms were, by this means, differentiating themselves in the market. Managers of public services might at first find it difficult to empathize with the way such values are expressed, but the need to be clear to staff, consumers and the public about what kind of organization you are is just as relevant as in private services.

Where do the values come from?

Values come in different shapes and sizes. Some, like equal opportunities and empowerment, are big, all-encompassing, difficult for anyone to disagree with but difficult to practice effectively and credibly. Others are more specific, relating to the particular position and role of an organization and the individuals working for it.

When trying to understand why particular values influence how 'quality' is interpreted and put into practice, it is as well to be aware of their different origins – political, managerial, professional, consumer or citizen – to see whether these match or conflict, and to compare what is *said* with what is *done*. Let us start with where the values are coming from.

Political, managerial and professional values

Local councillors are normally elected on a manifesto, itself derived from national political positions: their basic values are (partly) legitimated through the election process. In the rest of the public sector, 'Board' representatives are appointed, some from local authorities, some from voluntary organizations, increasing numbers from business, and a residue of the 'great and the good'. Whether elected or not, Board or Council level will be expected to work to 'political' values – with a small or a large 'p'. Mission or values statements at this level can be a useful guide for policy, or they may be regarded with scepticism. It depends how they are put into practice.

Then there are management values. People who are managers are not a race apart, though they may be seen as such by professionals. Nevertheless, even when appointed from a professional background such as health care or social work, different values begin to take priority once the management role is assumed. Public service managers do not *have* to espouse commercial values, but they will almost certainly be more concerned with the values of efficiency and economy then they had been used to. These can appear to conflict with other values such as sensitivity, flexibility and responsiveness. Whether these tensions can be handled constructively is likely to depend on the management style adopted, macho or otherwise.

'Professionalism' – always hard to define – can be viewed positively or negatively by the outside world. Traditional professional values are now being challenged, by new business practices, by the contract culture, by the removal of restrictive practices and by crises varying from child-care cases to corporate scandals. An optimistic recent definition of professionals suggests that they are:

> Responsible for their individual contributions to the business, which have a direct and major impact on its performance. Professionals are independent and autonomous. Whilst their main allegiance is to their professional discipline, their activities are controlled by a code of conduct which stresses that the interests of the 'client' are to be put before self-interest.
>
> (Watkins *et al.* 1992: 10)

If the key characteristic in professionals' relations with clients is trust, the key values are integrity and fair conduct. These values can be claimed as much by administrative, clerical and manual staff doing the job they are supposed to do as by those who claim professional status from qualifications and membership of a professional body. Such professionals may bring high quality, ethical standards and high levels of commitment to their employing organization. Or they may be seen as defensive, arrogant and protective of their status at the expense of the organization.

Consumer and citizen values

Consumers and citizens, given the chance to become involved in public service quality, bring with them a further, highly variable set of values. For some people, there may be strong elements of trust and faith in the professionals and 'the system'. For others, who have suffered from bad treatment in the past, or who know others who have, the value may be distrust and suspicion – 'don't let them get away with it'.

But the right to a decent, preferably high quality service, and the right to complain if the service is not good enough, is inalienable. These are the essential values of consumerism and citizenship, which may or may not be adopted by public service organizations. Altruistic professionals will also value users' complaints, to improve their services and as a check on their own power and authority.

Consensus and compromise

In any one organization, a wide range of values compete or coexist. Is consensus in fact necessary? If so, how can the values of minorities and undervalued groups (traditionally front-line staff, service users and social groups experiencing discrimination) be accommodated?

Two barriers to achieving consensus in the past have been departmentalism and hierarchical bureaucracies. Now 'short-termism' and externally imposed competitive structures tend to work against co-operation and consensus. However, agreement is not always possible or even desirable. Real differences can exist, which need to be acknowledged and understood. An organization whose values are to maximize profits, or to eliminate variation, will be less likely to acknowledge or, indeed, welcome, differences of any kind. It may look for consensus even where none is possible, ignoring minority rights in the process. Where quality is about conformity, this is a real danger. Disappointment may be experienced when agreement cannot be reached, yet there are many occasions when the solution is to 'agree to disagree'.

Some influential values

I want now to look at some of those values affecting how public service quality is defined and put into effect, though they do not relate just to service quality. Some of these values are treated by other writers (Centre for the Evaluation of Public Policy and Practice 1992; Local Government Management Board 1992) as integral to the definition of quality. However, I argue (in Chapter 3) for restricting the definition of quality to what cannot be defined as anything else. These values are:

- The three E's of economy, efficiency and effectiveness.
- Equity, equality and environment.
- Democracy, accountability, empowerment and community.
- Diversity, standardization and choice.
- Integration and specialization.
- Intervention and non-intervention.
- Competition and profit.

Economy, efficiency and effectiveness

Economy, efficiency, and effectiveness may be values or they may be merely management or accountancy tools. Because they influence how organizations behave, and how they approach the question of quality, I see them as underlying values.

In the early 1980s it was a struggle to get anything other than 'value for money' onto the public agenda. The ideals of economy (least cost inputs) and efficiency (highest outputs in proportion to inputs, or unit costs) were apparently displacing public sector values such as fairness and altruism. 'Effectiveness' can be defined as the achievement of objectives and (possibly) increasing the 'public good'. However, it was a less powerful value than the first two, largely because of the (continuing) difficulty of devising suitable measures for it (Audit Commission 1989). Quick turnover and cheapness seemed to be the order of the day.

So economy, efficiency and effectiveness need to be differentiated from each other. Where economy values are emphasized, high turnover and quick throughput will be the name of the game. Where effectiveness goals are emphasized, the impact of the service over a longer period than a single accounting year will be the prime consideration.

Equity and equality

Julian Le Grand and Ray Robinson suggested (1984: 2) that one of society's objectives is to distribute the goods and services it produces in a just and fair way. By the end of their book, *The economics of social problems*, they concluded that no universal definition of equity existed. At that stage, they detected two strands: equal treatment for equal need and the achievement of minimum standards in any one area of activity. In a later publication (Bramley and Le Grand 1992), equity was being seen more specifically in terms of *distribution*, which can be measured and monitored: who actually uses services and who does not? This is the sense in which it will be used here.

Equality – of opportunity and of access – focuses on needs and rights. An organization with a strong value of equality will make sure it knows the needs of all those whom its services are intended to benefit. It will actively acknowledge the right of all its citizens, including those generally under-represented within the decision-making structures, to make demands, complaints and suggestions about services. It will be concerned for its own staff, ensuring that its composition reflects the local population, and acknowledging the rights and needs of employees.

In summary, equality means that you make every effort to ensure that people *can* obtain the services they need, while equity emphasizes what people *do* obtain. Both are intimately linked with the question of 'whose quality'? An organization that does not have values of equity and equality will have a different view of who should be consulted, involved and responded to from one that does have those values.

Environmental values

An organization that values its environment will judge all its activities for their effect on both the quality of life of residents and on the sustainability of the physical environment.

Environmental values have three aspects. First, awareness, education and information: recognizing how little we know about the effects of our individual and collective actions on the environment, a willingness to assess the current position, and enabling others to assess your organization's practice. Second, understanding that environmental maintenance and improvement is a long-term and apparently expensive project: the benefits will not necessarily be directly to the organization, and may be felt by future generations rather than by current citizens. Third, public sector organizations may need to implement their commitment to environmental values, not through direct control but by persuasion and example.

Such values can be a way of demonstrating respect for the local inhabitants: street furniture – litter bins, telephone booths – on peripheral or inner city estates being of the same quality as those in the town centre; people being made to feel safe to walk in any part of the area; traffic calming and recycling schemes being discussed with all residents' and interest groups, not just with those whose members can 'speak the language'.

'The clean, green and safe town' policy – the management of open spaces, the maintenance and renewal of its urban fabric – was explicitly part of Harlow District Council's approach to quality: 'Cleanliness, safety and a passionate concern for the environment are the hallmarks of this service area'. (*Moving forward in 1990–91 and Beyond*, Harlow District Council May 1990). In other areas, 'thinking globally, acting locally' could produce partnerships between local authorities, central government (or the European Union) and the public to develop environmental audits, waste disposal and recycling schemes, house insulation and tree-planting. Local planning applications can be assessed for their environmental gain, just as they are sometimes assessed for their planning gain.

Democracy, accountability, empowerment and community

The fragmentation of the public sector makes it more and more difficult to guess where the lines of public accountability lie, and whether they involve a democratic dimension. At the level of central government, ministers can avoid being questioned on the grounds that 'operational' matters are the responsibility of the Chief Executive of the Next Steps agencies. Locally, more and more services are being contracted to 'providers', whose only answerability lies in the contract itself, not to the public or its elected representatives.

Yet unelected bodies can feel accountable to the public and their local community. Before the National Health Service changes, several community health units, in North Staffordshire for example, and in Exeter (Day 1990) set up neighbourhood forums, where a range of local professionals and members of the public could find out about and put points to their locality manager. Some Training and Enterprise Councils are trying to develop relations with the community through working parties and subcommittees. Consultation is very hard to get right (Gaster and Taylor 1993): the fact that such forums do not always succeed does not mean that they were cynical or tokenistic – although that can sometimes be the case.

In contrast, councillors, once elected, often claim to have a civic super-ego: this enables them to know what is needed without having to ask. It was to counter this 'we know best' attitude that the idea of the public service orientation was developed (Clarke and Stewart 1987). So it can go either way. Day and Klein (1987: 240), in their study of accountability, concluded:

> If members' perceptions of accountability are largely shaped by inter-nalised feelings of a duty and an ability to explain and justify, as suggested by our evidence, election is not a necessary condition for bringing this about.

Public service quality based on an ethos that stresses public accountability and democracy, that actively tries to involve consumers and citizens, will feel very different from a purely managerial process – which is what very many 'quality initiatives' are.

Diversity, standardization and choice

The red tape and bureaucracy that have characterized many public sector institutions is not, of course, confined to the public sector. Monopolies exist in the private sector and, even where there is competition, once inside a bureaucratic machine (think of your bank), there is often little room for manoeuvre. There is a great temptation for large organizations to use standardized procedures because it makes things simple and, in the short run, cheaper.

Standardization in the public sector used to be justified on the grounds that it is fair – 'we treat everyone in the same way'. If there was variation, it might mean that some people would get a better service than others or, put another way, that some people would get a *worse* service than others. This, in a publicly accountable body, was thought not to be acceptable.

Now it is recognized that treating everyone in a standard way can be very unfair. People's real needs differ enormously, and they react to similar treatment in quite different ways. Responsiveness to needs and sensitivity to and respect for people as individuals are now seen as essential ingredients for many areas of public service. They ought to lead to flexibility, choice and – the logical consequence – variation. The question is how to balance these new values with the old ones of fairness and equity.

How does this square with policies of zero defects and the elimination of non-conformance? Both have strong connotations of maximizing standardization, thereby reducing choice and flexibility. Processes of quality assurance and quality control run the risk (here's a paradox) that they will discourage risk-taking and, like performance indicators, focus all effort on achieving the norm: it is difficult to reconcile this approach with the sensitivity and responsiveness that are supposedly the acme of public sector quality.

Integration and specialization

In the 1970s, social services went generic. There had been too much specialization and separation between complementary services, too much duplication and yet too many gaps through which people could fall. At the same time, these and other services were decentralized (Gaster and Hoggett 1993), aiming to counteract territorialism of all kinds and to achieve, through more flexible working, multidisciplinary teams and joint, interagency projects, an integrated service for local people. For this, new kinds of skills were needed, to build networks and achieve effective collaboration and co-operation. An organization pursuing integrative values needed 'reticulators' – people who use networks to solve problems and meet needs (Webb 1991).

Pressures from central government legislation and the contract culture may now be reversing that trend. The perceived need to specify all aspects of work in the minutest detail leaves little room for flexibility and initiative among the workforce. The move towards a business culture could (and is) pushing towards respecialization and possibly, through the development of larger units intended to achieve greater purchasing power, to recentralization too.

For members of the public needing services, and for employees themselves, the difference between the specialist and the integrative, devolved ethos can be very striking. If an indicator of the two approaches is needed, it would be the different responses to a request for help, particularly one that does not fit neatly into an existing organizational pigeonhole. An organization with a specialist tendency will be one that passes people backwards and forwards between departments. In an integrative organization, staff will have been trained and have the personal commitment to find out for themselves what to do and then to do it.

Services are delivered through an interconnected and interdependent chain of actions. These chains can be short or long. The complexity of most public services highlights the necessity of understanding these chains and of ensuring that the links within them are clear and strong. This is what quality is about. So the more integrated the organization, the better the service is likely to be. The array of forces against integration and towards fragmentation underlines the need for an explicit organizational value of integration.

Intervention and non-intervention

For a decade and a half privatization, enforced contracts and the removal of key services from the sphere of democratically elected representatives have appeared to deny the role of the state in the direct provision of public services. At the same time, large areas of public service, notably higher and further education, opted out schools and hospital trusts, have been transferred from local control to that of central government. Any organization responsible for services to the public needs to think through the extent to which the state (central or local) has a right or a duty to intervene in its citizens' affairs. Should it adopt an interventionist or a more *laissez-faire* set of values?

In local government and the health service, in employment training and other central government agencies, the enabling, commissioning or purchaser role can be pursued in different ways. One way is to leave the market to sort itself out. Another, through partnerships with local communities and other agencies, is to develop profiles of need and to encourage the development and maintenance of services that might otherwise never get off the ground or survive, using grants, positive action, geographical targeting or other forms of support.

It would be unwise to assume that stereotypes exist as to how different organizations will behave. Labour- and Conservative-controlled local author-ities can both decide that their own services are or are not worth keeping. Some traditional Labour councils hang on grimly to all the services they can, some Conservative councils have divested themselves of direct provision as far as they could. But many Labour Councils have not sought to defend hopeless direct service organizations, while the then Conservative Councils of Hertfordshire and Bedfordshire worked in the early 1990s to develop relations with the other councils in their area, pooling resources so as to provide better services for the community (Gaster and Taylor 1993).

Competition and profit

One final set of values needs to be considered and then we have done. The question is, can public service organizations driven by the need to maximize income and minimize expenditure (and, if they are provider organizations, to gain a larger share of the market) yet remain true to the public sector ethos, however that might be defined?

Equity, equality, concern and altruism are all part of the 'public sector ethos' but, except possibly for equity, they are not confined to the public sector. Philanthropic works generally start from voluntary and private effort. Some private companies are committed to equality in their employment prac-tices. Private and voluntary organizations delivering public services under con-tract are likely to display the widest possible range of values (Taylor *et al.* 1994).

It is the compatibility of these values that is the vital issue. Does the concern for profits and market share drive out other values that are essential ingredients of public sector service quality? What, in the world of quasi-markets, is the role of the client or purchaser in holding on to *public* values while employing *private* organizations to deliver the services?

Values and objectives

Values, then, are a key component in considering quality. From values, objectives can be derived. It is the combination of these that defines the 'business' that public service organizations are in. That is the starting point for thinking about the nature of the services, the definition of their quality and how it is to be measured (see Figure 1.1).

At the same time, the values driving the organization dictate the processes it employs – the process of policy implementation and the process of developing standards and of measuring achievement. Some basic differences are: (1) between values that lead to involvement in and ownership of policies, and those that generate fear, distrust or cynicism; (2) between values that encourage co-operation, teamwork and working with difference, and those that foster competitiveness, individualism and standardization; (3) between values that look good on paper and those that are actually practised. If these latter are different, particularly at the top levels of policy and management, it is difficult for good practice lower down the organization to flourish or to be built on. The organizational culture is inimical to good service quality. Too much depends on the personal values of individual staff, quality is patchy and the public has no idea what it can reasonably expect of the service.

The process of developing and publicly expressing objectives is one way of helping people know what to expect – and of helping staff know what they should do. These objectives – sometimes externally imposed, sometimes homegrown – derive from values, even if these are not explicit. They are part of the rational model of management, providing clear directions for the organization. They can both guide the definition of quality being aimed at, and form a baseline for diagnosing whether it can be or is being achieved. Strategic objectives are a necessary part of the quality cycle.

Many public sector organizations (and those agencies providing public services through the contract process) now develop strategy statements, business plans, statements of purchasing intentions or strategic objectives called by any other name. Such objectives may cover the organization's role in the local community, they will take account of legal and financial constraints and they will normally reflect any agreed priorities of politicians and managing boards. Strategic policies provide important clues in the search to define what services are for – the 'fitness for purpose' of quality.

They can also provide a basis for accountability and, by providing a starting point for internal planning, they provide a framework within which flexibility and discretion can be exercised. If the culture is right, strategic objectives can even legitimate 'risky' actions, cutting through long-winded procedures and achieving quite radical improvements in a service. If they are not clear, and the culture is hierarchical or individualistic, the temptation is to 'cover one's back', just in case.

Timescales for implementation: success and failure

Evaluative research about whether objectives have been achieved often comes up against problems of disappointed expectations. One of the most common reasons for this is that not enough time is allowed. In a blaming culture, scapegoats are sought, or else an experiment is pronounced a failure before it has had time to become a success.

Yet strategic objectives are, by definition, long term. Even where the 'big bang' approach is taken, with massive change apparently taking place overnight, structures (if restructuring is involved, as it usually is) may change quite quickly, but cultures and attitudes take far longer. New structures can speed things up, but only if it is clear what they are for – what is to be achieved by the new structure that could not be done with the old? Except in those rare organizations where change is the norm and the culture is receptive to new ideas, a new strategy's impact on service users and the community is never as quick as its initiators hoped.

Strategies to improve quality are long-term strategies, developing over three to five years or even longer. Time is not the only success factor, but it seems that few organizations, in the public or private sectors, make enough allowance for quality objectives to be jointly developed, analysed and allowed to take root. Too often they are 'evaluated' out of existence.

Central and local strategic objectives

Strategy is often equated with 'the centre'. Policy units tend to be at the centre, committees operate centrally, so do management boards and the like. With the increasing interest in devolved management, and revived interest in decentralization and localization, strategy can be developed at a number of levels.

Studies of decentralized organizations in health and local government show the need for the area manager and area committee to take a lead in evolving *local* strategies (Gaster *et al.* 1992; Ham 1992). These, like corporate or central strategies, need to be placed within a framework of values, they need to take a long- or medium-term view, and they need to be operationally possible. The advantage is that they can respond to local needs and involve more people, especially local residents, in their construction. But the first step is for the centre to acknowledge the locality's or devolved unit's strategic role, and it is here that some unnecessary tensions arise: central policy staff may feel sidestepped, while local managers may feel that local knowledge is not being used.

This centre–local tension is illustrated as far as quality is concerned by the issue of who should set standards. Standard-setting is perhaps a half-way point between setting broad strategic objectives, and the detailed action that is needed to make that thinking a reality.

Conclusions

It is increasingly difficult to talk about 'quality in the public sector', or even 'quality in public services': what is or is not a public service is harder than ever to define, while the debate on the nature and process of quality is moving at an alarming speed. The fact that the subject is in such a state of flux makes it all the more important to be clear what has happened so far, what are the main features of quality in the early 1990s, and what are the pressures and constraints that face managers trying to implement quality programmes in the future.

This first chapter has set the scene for a more detailed look at the main dimensions of quality – its definition, its implementation and its measurement. I have introduced a model for considering quality which should help readers to make the links between what have largely been separate recipes and debates. While no more prescriptive than any rational model can ever be, it does suggest a way of approaching the rather daunting issue of 'where do I start', as well as underlining the need to involve not just managers, but a whole range of interests at each stage.

As a launch pad for defining quality, the second half of this chapter focused on values – values on paper and values in practice – and the strategic objectives that, if not explicit, leave quality floating in space. Knowing your values and objectives provides the starting point for saying what a service must do. Defining quality is, then, the next step.

2

Whose quality?

The way quality is defined and the question of who is doing the defining are intimately connected. Definitions are important: they drive the whole implementation process and are the basis of standard setting and measurement. But to treat them as quasi-scientific objective facts, as the language of 'conformance to specification' and 'fitness for purpose' appears to do, or to couch them in terms of customer satisfaction, does not capture the essence of what public service quality is all about.

Not everyone is a customer, and not everyone can be satisfied. We need a definition (or, rather, definitions) that takes account of the different roles of those with an interest in public services, and can appropriately counterbalance the traditional power of organizations and professionals. Public accountability and the very real restrictions on consumer choice make the process of defining service quality in the public sector far more complicated than in the private sector making goods, where much of the language of quality originated.

The main question, it seems to me, is how to balance the complex needs, wants and demands of individuals, communities and society as a whole, with the capacity, resources, legal requirements and technical abilities of organizations and individuals responsible for achieving good quality services.

Quality definitions cannot be imposed, but need to emerge from a process of negotiation. This does not have to be a bipartite confrontation between two opposing sides. Ideally, it should be a constructive discussion between key parties who know and acknowledge each other's needs and limitations. Negotiating definitions is in itself a process, sometimes long drawn out. Within a secure framework of consultation and participation, it provides a natural starting point for deciding how to achieve the quality defined (the implementation methods), for setting targets and standards, and for developing suitable measurements and ways of measuring progress.

The reason for making so much of values in the last chapter now becomes apparent. Despite some blurred boundaries of responsibility – between social services and health authorities in community care, between purchasers and providers, clients and contractors in respect of service monitoring – in most situations it is reasonably clear who has the last word. This is so even where the increasingly misleading language of 'partnership' is used. So if one agency has the ultimate right and responsibility, as enabler or purchaser, to decide the level, nature and quality of its services, what if any rights can be exercised by others, especially those individuals and communities directly or indirectly affected by its services? What are the organizational and political values that both influence the quality of negotiation and determine the strategic objectives from which service priorities are derived?

An organization that professes to values of equality or respect – as many public service organizations do – but then fails to listen to its staff and service users or, by the way it behaves (its culture), prevents women, people from black and ethnic minorities, disabled people or gay people from feeling welcome and confident, loses credibility. In the late 1980s, as a result of the 1988 Housing Act, many housing departments – Birmingham among them – announced a 'customer care' policy. In the hierarchical, bureaucratic culture that the Birmingham Housing Department then was, staff (especially those in other departments) were extremely cynical about a policy that appeared to be a knee-jerk reaction to national legislation but failed to think about staff care or the interdepartmental co-operation that would make the policy a reality (Gaster 1991b). How, in this instance, would the quality of housing services be defined?

Similarly, in 1992, after much pressure from the local Voluntary Services Council, the top-level Wolverhampton joint community care planning group invited representatives from black and ethnic minority organizations to join the six client-based care planning teams. The clash of cultures and values in social services and the health authority dominated the planning process. The real practical difficulties of small, fragile and marginally funded groups was not acknowledged, and group processes were not developed where representatives could feel comfortable or make their voice heard. The result, at least in the short term, was that the needs of the black community were not properly considered, despite the well-intentioned paper policy (Martin and Gaster 1993).

If, on the other hand, the stated values and those that are actually practised are consistent, there should be less of a problem in developing a credible way forward. In Harlow, with its decentralization and democratization programme, local residents' groups have been able to get their very local needs incorporated into local statements of environmental standards (Gaster 1995). In Wiltshire in 1993, the Social Services Department and the Health Authorities

signed a 'service level agreement' with the recently developed Wiltshire Community Care Users' Network, ensuring the latter's place in service planning
and delivery, in staff training and in monitoring (Martin 1993). In Newcastle,
largely through the enthusiasm and commitment of the contracts officer of the
purchasing health authority and of the Chief Executive of the Mental Health
Services Trust, the Mental Health Services Consumer Group gained a high
profile in both contract specification and service monitoring (Harrison 1993).

In each of these cases, an infrastructure was being established where the
detailed consideration of quality definitions could begin. The organizational
values of those with power, the statutory authorities, enabled this to happen.

Because of the importance of not allowing quality definitions to be
producer dominated, it seems right to think about who are the 'customers',
what other interests (or, in the currently fashionable language, 'stakeholders')
may want or have a right to be involved, and what processes may help or
hinder the definition of quality by negotiation. This precedes the discussion of
different ways of defining quality in the next chapter.

Stakeholders and interests

My aim at this point is to think as widely as possible about who might, at some
stage of a service, want or need to become engaged in defining service quality. It
is important not to limit the debate to active participants (as the language of user–
involvement and consumerism does) and as a generic term I prefer the word
'interest' to 'stakeholder'. The latter is, I think, tainted with a kind of commer-
cialism inappropriate for public services, though a quick hunt through the in-
dexes of books by private sector gurus such as Deming, Crosby, Oakland and
Peters and Waterman shows that it is not a word used in their language, anyway.

Interests can coincide – they can be synergistic, working together to
produce more than the sum of the parts. If, however, there are major differences in culture, language, priorities or purposes, one of the elements in a
negotiation is to recognize and live with the differences as well as to note the
areas of common concern. Interests can also be oppressed and repressed: it then
becomes the job of the manager to uncover those interests and enable them to
be expressed (Williamson 1992).

The whole world cannot be involved in negotiations. Some parties (the
Audit Commission – or the electorate) are interested only in results. Nevertheless, for any one service, a surprisingly long list of interests can be constructed.

Users, non–users, carers: the need to differentiate

Once public services begin to be seen as intended to benefit the public, however defined and however disparate the points of view, it is right and proper
that people in their role as consumers and citizens are brought into the debate
at an early stage. Public services come in several broad categories, which bring
with them different kinds of relationships between service providers and the

public. Only the last category in the following list could be said to have 'customers'.

- Some services are provided to everyone – universal services such as street sweeping, rubbish collection, environmental maintenance and improvements.
- Some services are demand-led (advice, information, primary health care).
- Some services are only available to those deemed eligible, according to legislation or locally determined rules (welfare benefits, council housing, shelter for the homeless).
- Other services are rationed by resource availability, or by decisions based on an assessment of 'need' (day-nursery places, home helps, most forms of health and social care).
- Some services are imposed through legislation, aiming to benefit or protect individuals or society or both (primary and secondary education; some social services – probation services, mental health services; food standards and health and safety; police and prisons).
- Some services are preventative, aiming to help people and communities help themselves, or to provide group support in order to pre-empt individual crises (community development and, generally, developmental – as opposed to reactive – services).
- For some services there are no eligibility requirements, they are available for all to use as they wish, sometimes for a charge. In order to avoid rationing by the purse, pricing policies may be devised to help particular groups use the facilities – the young, the old, the unemployed, the disabled (leisure services, libraries, transport).

Most public services fall into one or more of these categories. While there may be extra complications superimposed by the contracting-out process, the underlying nature of the services remains the same whether directly provided or 'enabled' through contracts.

In some services, consumers may have less to lose than others, or they may be able to pool their common strength to achieve change. In others, consumers are far more isolated and (literally) in the power of the service provider. In others again, consumers feel dependent on the services and would hesitate to criticize or even to ask questions, for fear that the service will be withdrawn.

There are relatively few services where people are treated as 'customers' in the traditional sense that they are paying for services *and* have a choice of whether or not to use the service. This is the only type of service that people can walk away from if they do not like it (the exit option), though it is also possible for customers to get together and make suggestions for improvement (the voice option).

There is, of course, no harm in thinking of people as customers if this means that they are going to be treated better. But better treatment does not arise simply from a new label: the rather widespread use of the word 'customer' should not be used to disguise the fact that most people have very different relationships with the public services. Consumerism may have made both producers and consumers more aware of the need to look for options *within* the service but, except for those who can afford to use private schools and medicine, exercising consumer influence by withdrawing custom and going elsewhere is not normally possible.

A point ignored by the legislation that gives existing parents the right to vote for their school to opt out of local authority control, or which gives Council tenants the right to vote for the property they live in to be removed from the public housing stock, is that there are vital differences of interest between current consumers and those who are not using the service. For example, they may not be using the service because they are not eligible or have been refused, or perhaps are on a waiting list; they may be unaware of their rights, ignorant of the service, or excluded through discrimination. They may be future or past users.

This may seem horribly complicated to the service provider, who is having to count the cost of involving consumers, in time and money. It may seem simpler to consult current users. However, if they are weak, inarticulate, young, old, poor, disturbed, geographically remote or being compelled to use the service, this too can make things difficult, possibly too difficult. Nevertheless it is important to try, and, with a bit of help and imagination, there are ways of going about it.

The People First movement has begun trying to remove the barriers of communication for people with learning difficulties. Some advocacy schemes have been supported, like the one run by Age Concern in Wolverhampton, where volunteers work to express the needs of old people and put pressure on the services to meet them; specialist interviewers were used in a National Consumer Council survey (1990) to find out what elderly people with dementia thought of the services they were receiving; the members of the Newcastle mental health group were 'survivors': they could not speak out while they were in mental hospitals, but they had plenty to say once they were out of the system.

The other temptation for service providers is to consult those who care for the actual users as a proxy for the users themselves. Carers form a very important set of interests, ignored until very recently. The Community Care Special Action Project, started in 1987, pioneered the idea that, in Birmingham, carers have views and needs of their own, separate from those of those they are looking after. The danger now is that, because health and social services are so dependent on the goodwill of carers as alternative or supplementary providers of care, they will forget to listen to the consumers themselves.

Carers may be thought to have more understanding of the service than is actually the case. This, too, has its dangers. Local planning groups for people with learning difficulties in North Wales included parents for some time before people who actually used the services became involved. This caused two difficulties. First, parents were more anxious than the consumers about trying out new things, for example regarding the use of day and residential facilities. They felt safer if their children were not 'in the community'. This caused problems for the professionals who were trying to introduce innovative ways of providing services that at first sight were distinctly more risky than the traditional ones. Second, the service providers did not realize that parents – carers – were no more used to jargon (what is 'normalization' in everyday language?) than were the patients, clients or consumers. A parent at a planning meeting said that she had not opened her mouth for a year, and that it was much easier after service users started coming, as the providers had then started talking plain English (Gaster and Taylor 1993).

Citizens

Through the process of judicial review, individual citizens can challenge decisions by statutory authorities. They derive this right from administrative law and from time to time they exercise it. However, it is a complex, expensive and time-consuming process, which is very much a last resort. Current discussions of citizenship suggest that citizens can be involved in services in a much more constructive, and a more continuous way. Nevertheless, there are many obstacles – far more, possibly, than stand in the way of direct consumers, whose rights in relation to particular services are less easily challenged.

Taylor *et al.* (1992) note that there are two kinds of 'right'. Procedural rights derive from a relationship with a particular service or element of the State. They seem mainly to be expressed through the right to *redress*. This leads to an emphasis on complaints procedures and the publication of information in the form of league tables in documents like the Citizen's Charter (HMSO 1991).

Substantive rights are those that 'emphasise the participation of the citizen in shaping the common purposes of society' (HMSO 1991). From these rights come *entitlements* to services, which may be received automatically, or they may have to be pursued more actively through various methods of participation and persuasion. The Citizen's Charter, which despite its name has in practice focused more on current users of services than on the wider notion of citizens in the community, nevertheless says in its introductory leaflet that:

> We all pay for our public services through our taxes. We therefore have a right to expect that they will do what their name suggests – serve the public.

The rights derived from citizenship are particularly important for excluded groups. They can base requests or demands for involvement, not on the patronage or kindness or liberalism of the service providers, but on their own rights. Beresford and Croft (1993: 18) quote people with learning difficulties or who are (or have been) mentally ill constantly being fobbed off on various grounds (lack of appropriate skills; unrepresentativeness): 'They just couldn't believe we could speak for ourselves.'

So it may be difficult for citizens to become involved in service quality. With the emphasis on consumers, and especially on current users, the democratic aspect of public services can easily be forgotten. An explicit commitment to citizen involvement is needed. Efforts to develop forums – neighbourhood and area forums, forums for the elderly or for ethnic minorities – have been made from time to time (Gaster and Taylor 1993). This has been in the context of policies to develop participative democracy and a better relationship with different groups within the community. The aim is to improve accountability and to empower those whose voice is not normally heard, to develop the notion of 'community government'. Such forums have been an effective and exciting way for officers and councillors to get to grips with the detail of how their services are perceived and to find out what is wanted. It can, however, be very exposing for those officers and councillors, who, in Area Committees as far apart as Harlow and South Somerset, literally have to face the audience, rather than talking to each other round a committee table. A programme of citizen involvement needs considerable investment, of community development and other support, and of time to enable consultation to take place. This can feel like an extra pressure for officers struggling with new contract processes, reduced resources and increased demand:

> In our experience managers and professionals in local government still see the public as a nuisance. They are perceived as a nuisance because the demands they make are unrealistic, because one group of citizens want one thing whereas another group wants something else, because they are parochial in their outlook, because they are often prejudiced and because they are never satisfied. In addition, most councillors, tenants' representatives and leaders of community groups are viewed as unrepresentative, self-seeking and unrealistic. Recognise such attitudes? Our guess is that most of you will see at least some of these feelings in yourself.
>
> (Hambleton and Hoggett 1990)

If more people become actively involved in decisions affecting society, it is not a bad thing for democracy. It takes time and courage for ordinary people to 'walk through the door'. My study of Liverpool neighbourhood centres showed how local people, who had never been formally involved, were able to provide support for neighbours who would not go near the statutory services, and at the same time gain strength and power to make local needs known and to campaign for (and get) extra resources for local use (Gaster 1993a). The support of a voluntary organization, the Personal Services Society, was crucial, but the centres could not have continued their existence, or gained local credibility, without the active involvement of people living 'just round the corner'.

Councillors and appointed Board members

If public service quality is to be a democratic policy, involving not just managers, but consumers and citizens too, then a driving force behind the definition and implementation of quality has to be the political values of the organization. These are held, respectively, by councillors and, in non-local-government agencies, by Board members.

It has been striking, in the contacts I have had with local authorities, that quality initiatives have generally been given their first impetus by managers: councillors have not been very visible in this debate. Yet councillors must have a part to play in the development of quality policies, in two ways. They, as the 'necessary centre' of local political authority (Benington and Taylor 1992), have direct responsibility for the quality of government. However, if local groups of consumers and residents are to be given more of a say between elections, through processes of consultation, participation and empowerment, what role does that leave for the councillor?

As the role of local government changes, so does that of the councillor. Not only are councillors elected and accountable representatives, they have also to hold the line for the common good and for public values such as fairness, equality, environment and the local economy, and for the longer-term future. This, in a society where fewer and fewer of those responsible for local services are also locally accountable, is an increasingly important role, characterized as 'community leadership' (Local Government Management Board 1993b). Councillors must make strategic decisions and develop policy; they can support and develop their local communities, in partnership with staff, consumers and local citizens; they can facilitate the exercise of citizen and consumer rights; and they can act as advocates – for people in the community and for the authority as a whole (Gaster and Taylor 1993).

Some of these roles equate with the 'downstream' role, as Benington and Taylor (1992: 178) called it, of 'observing and responding to the experience of workers and clients at the front line'. Others are the 'upstream' roles corresponding to the strategic management role of officers: setting objectives and targets, mobilizing resources and monitoring results. There is enormous potential for councillors to make significant contributions at both levels if they are willing and able to separate out these two aspects of their role. They are perhaps the only people who can legitimately bridge the gap between policy and practice, and who have the power to bring about change. It is ultimately the councillors, in local government, who have the power *and* the responsibility to make the policy decisions on which the whole system rests.

Little has so far been written about the 'new magistracy' of Board members (but see Davis and Stewart 1993), particularly regarding their effect on the day to day work of their organizations and the promotion of quality in their services. In lieu of direct democracy, these are the people who, however they were appointed, now have responsibility to the community. They have power over an increasing number of public services, as direct providers (Next Steps agencies such as the Benefits Agency), as purchasers of services from other organizations (Health Authorities, Training and Enterprise Councils) and as contractors (National Health Service Trusts, opted-out schools and the whole range of public, private and voluntary organizations bidding for tenders).

In the past, some of these appointees did feel a sense of accountability to the public. However, the public is not acknowledged to have the right to hold them to account. Board and management committee members may be appointed to represent a particular constituency – the local authority for example – or particular interests, such as black and ethnic minorities. Such Board members can be placed in a very awkward position, constrained by commercial confidentiality from reporting back to those they are expected to represent, losing credibility in the process. A 1993 study of Training and Enterprise Councils' policies for people from ethnic minorities (Employment Department 1994) illustrated how difficult it was for black Board members either to affect policy or to relate to their local black communities. They were caught between two stools.

If this was the experience of a group of Board members who, in most instances, felt a keen sense of accountability to the part of the community they were representing, how much more difficult for Board members with no such natural constituency.

Front-line workers

Quality policies have tended to be very top-down, both in the private and the public sector, whether because of the gurus' maxim that top management should themselves be committed (passionate?), or simply because that is how they have always done things. A group that tends to be forgotten is the employees at the interface with the public, working with consumers and citizens.

As Lipsky (1980) pointed out, and my own experience as a front line manager and in subsequent research confirmed, in a hierarchical culture the interests of the front-line staff are different from those of staff in other parts of the organization. Devolved decision-making and the flatter organizational structures increasingly favoured as part of effective public management could in time reduce some of the tensions. But involvement of front-line staff – the street-level bureaucrats – is important because they have probably the most accurate idea *within* the organization of the concerns of current consumers. If they are community-minded, or are natural networkers, as many front-line managers are, they will have a wider view of the needs and expectations of the communities they serve.

Recognizing and valuing front-line staff is important and overdue. Otherwise front-line staff may simply transmit their own feeling of helplessness to the public (James 1989). This does not mean that their views can in any way be taken to represent those of consumers and citizens. Whatever front-line staff report about consumers will have been filtered through their own values, perceptions and experience, positive and negative. As an interest group, however, they need to be regarded and listened to, in conjunction with other key groups within and outside the organization.

Trade union interests

If quality is to improve, then changes in work practices and procedures are inevitable: otherwise, the public services would already be of high quality.

Trades unions are often neglected in the discussion and practice of quality. Their effect can be negative *or* positive.

Unions' interest in the well-being of staff can sometimes override that of consumers, in appearance and in practice. Many of the decentralization initiatives of radical urban Labour councils in the early 1980s – intended to provide a structure for service improvement – were slowed down or brought to a complete halt through union action (Miller 1991). In a period of major change, where jobs are under constant threat and hard-won skills appear to be challenged, industrial relations have to be particularly constructive if quality policies are not to be seen as yet another attack on public service workers. Quality policies ought to affect the whole organization. However, the impact, particularly when they are couched in terms of 'customer care', will possibly be felt first at the front line. Here, employees are worst paid and most powerless. It is not surprising if trades unions take up protective (and apparently defensive) positions, especially if they have not been consulted early enough (Ashrif 1993).

The challenge of the 1988 Local Government Act, which widened compulsory competitive tendering to include refuse collection, street cleaning and grounds maintenance, galvanized the public sector unions into seeing quality as part of the competitive edge for direct service organizations (Paddon 1992). The idea that providing a high quality service might not only preserve public sector jobs but also increase job satisfaction and appreciation from the public – and, in the longer run, keep down costs through less re-work – may increase union commitment and understanding in the field of policies. It all depends on how the policies are introduced.

Relations can, then, be positive. Full, constructive discussion is possible about the likely impact of quality policies on job descriptions and work practices. Negotiation is possible about phasing, training and ring-fencing. Unions do not have to feel 'co-opted' to be actively involved.

Managers and professionals

One of the positive aspects of professionalism is the ability to think freshly about professional goals and values, and to welcome, anticipate or initiate change. Similarly, managers can take up new ideas and become the 'change agents', leading an organization into new ways of thinking and behaving.

These are often people coming new to an organization, who were not caught up in the old ways and who have nothing to lose (no stake) in the past. But they may, too, be people who felt suffocated under the old regime and now have a chance to try out their own ideas and to develop new skills. Devon Social Services, which first decentralized in 1987, decided in 1993 to make a split between the purchasing and providing roles within the department and to devolve budgets to the lowest possible level. This meant that some of its eighty or so team managers, working in nineteen districts, were by 1994 handling million pound community care budgets. At the same time they were having to support their teams to move away from direct provision to assessment and monitoring roles. Because of the heavy managerial pressures, new practice supervisors were to be appointed, dividing the management and professional roles for the first time.

The practice supervisors were the people who would in practice be defining quality both for the organization and for service users. Devon, with a system of green and white papers, had developed processes of internal consultation. But could managers and professionals be effectively involved? They were reeling under the impact of the new legislation and from the effects of the throughput mentality of health trusts, which, through early discharge policies, put ever greater demands on social and community health services. Yet if they were *not* involved, could the standards of care being developed for day and residential services ever be meaningful?

Balancing the interests: a question of power and participation

If defining quality is a matter of negotiation, it might be assumed that, once the main interest groups are defined, each will have more or less equal power. This is patently not the case.

Power comes from different sources: from position – Board member, senior officer, recognized community leader – legitimized in some way through appointment or election; from professional status and from the positive or negative strength of individual personalities – a leader or a bully. There is also the power of credibility based on past performance, power derived from citizen and consumer rights, the power of knowledge and the power of the collectivity. This last is the power that, in relation to public services, consumer and residents' groups have been building for the last thirty years. It is particularly important because it can help combat the fragilities of some interest groups, especially consumers, which inherently have less power than others.

Stigma, dependence, deference, lack of self-esteem, discrimination (or fear of it), lack of support or recognition and lack of a legitimate power base are more or less the obverse of these sources of power. Several of these weaknesses also affect front-line staff and managers, voluntary and community organizations and even back-bench councillors.

There is an increasing literature about the principles and practice of consultation and participation (see, for example, Beresford and Croft 1993; Gaster and Taylor 1993; Smith 1992). Anyone involved in improving quality in the public services needs to be well educated in these matters. Identifying key interest groups, enabling them to be involved effectively and redressing imbalances of power are all part of the process of developing a suitable organizational culture for quality.

Perhaps the most important aspect of participation policies – and the easiest to get wrong – is the need to be clear about how much, if any, power is in fact to be shared. Will there be real listening, or in some cases joint decision-making, between the different interests, especially by those with the ultimate power of decision? In the end, it is up to the public service organization to balance the range of views, demands, suggestions, expressions of need, against each other, against its own power of performance (resources, technical skills, legal requirements) and against baseline values such as equity, equality and concern for the environment. At the same time, potential participants have to make their own decisions about whether the effort of getting involved is worth it. Will there be any results? So each forum or consultation process needs to be integrated with formal decision-making mechanisms, otherwise it will be marginalized and eventually unsupported.

Managers may develop good ideas and networks for participation but feel at a loss, far from the skills they were trained to use. Local government staff are possibly more versed in some aspects of consultation (though there is a long way to go). In the health services, under pressure from the community care legislation to consult the community, almost no relevant experience exists. Some local health forums do exist, patient and user surveys are quite common (Everitt 1990), the self-help movement, which contains pressure groups, has been going for some time. Yet Pat Taylor, in her survey of consumers, self-help groups and health professionals in the Swindon area, found that:

> Strategies [for consultation] have been formulated by managers and their implementation has been top-down. Direct health professionals have often been left uncertain and anxious about their roles. In general, health professionals have been trained to give a direct service to people in need and encouraged to develop clear job boundaries. This does not make it easy for new ways of working to be developed which includes stronger partnerships with other agencies, voluntary groups or with the consumer directly.
>
> (Taylor 1991: 4)

Ground rules are important: how to run a meeting, how to deal with conflict, how to network and ensure equal participation, how to support weaker or more powerless groups. There is a whole range of new skills that public service managers and service practitioners will need for the management of quality, on top of the ability to deliver the service to the required standard.

Quality cannot be left to the managers

Policies to improve quality are often perceived as an attempt – well-meaning or cynical, according to interpretation – by managers of services to the public to improve their image and be more responsive to the needs and demands of current service users. This chapter has demonstrated the need to think far more widely, and less passively, about what role a whole series of interests may play in the development and maintenance of such policies.

Thinking about service users, the first thing to be aware of is that their relationships to service providers varies greatly. Users receiving services forced on them by regulation or by the wider needs of the whole community, and users receiving services they depend on for their survival, are in a much weaker position to argue about and challenge the nature of those services than users of services where there was some choice, or which do not affect day to day life in quite such an intimate way. Some people use services for the very reason that they are weak and vulnerable – through illness or learning disability, or because of past experience of discrimination and stereotyping – and simply do not have the ability or strength on their own to assert and if necessary fight for their rights. Yet at the same time, caution needs to be used when consulting with proxy users, such as carers or professional advocates.

Beyond the complexities of consulting with direct users – consultation is a much better way of finding out what people want of you than merely waiting to see who actually uses the services – the importance of finding out the needs and views of a whole range of other groups and individuals with a legitimate interest in the nature and quality of the service becomes apparent. The role of politicians is particularly significant, as a counter-balance to the dominance of managers and, in some cases, professionals, in determining the day to day quality of a service. In the search for improvement, the constructive involvement of trades unions and front-line staff is also crucial to the successful implementation of quality policies.

Finally, I have suggested in this chapter that organizations responsible for services to the public, whether as clients or contractors, purchasers or providers, or in other roles such as community leaders, need to pay attention to the processes of involving the range of interests identified. Imbalances of power need to be addressed through positive action of various kinds. Consultation and participation with the public and with staff, for example, cannot, if it is to avoid being labelled as tokenistic, be undertaken without some serious investment of time and effort. Understanding the complex processes of effective consultation and embarking on the learning curve of participation is hard and potentially frustrating, as we know from the experience of the local authorities that have tried to develop a more participative style. Yet if the definitions and, eventually, the implementation and evaluation of quality is not in practice to be dominated by the old bureaucracies, a change in the organizational culture – allowing and encouraging a more open, informative and learning style – is part of the essential infrastructure for quality.

3

What quality?

Are definitions possible?

Having spent the last chapter discussing who should be party to the process of defining quality (and to much else – most of the 'interests' I have identified will also have parts to play in the rest of the quality cycle shown in Figure 1.1), I now need to turn to the issue of actual definitions.

No single, or simple definitions of quality exist. Everyone writing about it, or trying to practise it, has to struggle to come up with a working proposition, with which others are only too likely to disagree. Sometimes the difficulty is that the definition is too broad, so that it becomes meaningless: it cannot be put straight into practice. Others go for detail which, while possibly appropriate to a particular service, is difficult to generalize to all public services.

It seems to me that there are three fundamental sorts of definitions:

1 Definitions that try to encapsulate the nature of a service, breaking it down into a variety of quality dimensions (Donabedian 1980; Stewart and Walsh 1989; Walsh 1991).
2 Definitions that focus more on process. They take as their starting point the differences between the perceptions and the experiences of consumers, expressed in the notion of 'satisfaction'. Quality, or lack of it, is identified as the mismatches – the gaps – both within the organization and between it and its public (Maister 1985; Parasuraman et al. 1985). Quality is about closing those gaps.
3 Consumer-led definitions that, explicitly or by implication, highlight the question of which people and groups ought to be taken into account. In

total quality management language, these definitions talk about 'delighting' the customer (Joss *et al.* 1991). They imply a negotiated definition of quality, by referring to the need to meet 'agreed needs' (Centre for the Evaluation of Public Policy and Practice 1992). They may see the *active* involvement of consumers as desirable and, in a democratic definition of quality, some definitions see citizens as the primary reference group (Pfeffer and Coote 1991).

A combination of ideas

Each of these three approaches can be helpful. They combine the idea of being quite specific about the characteristics needed (which could be producer-dominated), with the need for the service to be satisfactory (consumer-orientated), while these two perspectives can be combined through the recognition that, with a wide range of needs to be satisfied, some characteristics need to be traded off against others: the final definition has to be agreed through some process of negotiation.

From here, a definition of quality with practical utility for a wide range of public services could be developed. The details of each service will be different, but each should be able to demonstrate:

- The characteristics of service quality defined in certain key dimensions.
- Understanding of the gap between expectations and experience of a service – the 'satisfaction' gap.
- The identification of key interests, including those of citizens and direct and indirect consumers, of staff, managers, professionals and politicians.

I am not sure that at this stage I am ready to come up with a neat formulation to define quality, nor that one is absolutely necessary. It is a framework, not a memorable (or unmemorable) phrase that I am after. Slogans can be alienating and they can stop people from thinking things out for themselves. In its relatively short life in the public sector, even the word 'quality' is in danger of becoming just such a slogan, so there seems little point in adding yet another phrase to this unwanted vocabulary.

In addition, some of the formulations that already exist do not seem particularly appropriate for public services. This is partly because they were developed with manufacturing in mind, where the costs of quality can more easily be counted, and where products, whether customized or mass produced, are manufactured in large enough quantities for standardization to be a key requirement around which the notion of quality revolves.

Such formulations are also inappropriate because they were evolved for private sector companies, which are likely to have different sets of values and objectives, even if many are now involved in the provision of public services through contracts. The key difference is the profit motive, but this is not the only one (see Stewart and Walsh 1992 for a useful review of private sector techniques and their suitability to public services).

When trying to define quality, I try to keep it to the minimum, as I said in Chapter 1. I see service quality as *consisting* of essential characteristics and of being *influenced* by other factors and values. These latter would normally require separate programmes for their management and implementation. The connections between the quality characteristics and the factors assisting or undermining their achievement need to be as clear as possible. When thinking about the characteristics of a particular service, I generally try to apply a test along the lines of:

- Would this aspect of service be improved or changed *without* a quality policy?
- What *other* service characteristics (e.g. efficiency, equality) are needed to ensure improvement of service quality?

The nature of public service quality

What is it that people actually want from a public service – a service they may choose to receive, may apply to receive, *or* may be forced to receive? When people can vote about their services – that is, for services provided by or through local and central government – are they thinking about the quality of existing services, or are they more interested in quantity, cost and priorities? Insofar as they are interested in quality, what are the distinguishing features they (we) are looking for? Are they looking for different things according to the type of service, or are there some common characteristics pervading all services?

Other aspects may be important. For example, does it make a difference who is the provider of the service – whether it is the core organization or a contractor? If the service does all that the consumer hopes it will do, then it may appear not to matter. If things go wrong, or if information is being sought, then maybe it does matter. Access to the accountable elected body, or possibly to an appointed board may be relatively simple. Access to third-party providers, whose link may be at several removes from the electorate, is likely to be more difficult. Contractors, sheltering behind their contract and notions of commercial confidentiality, may be reluctant either to give an account of their actions or to respond to complaints. However, access to the apparently more accountable bodies may be just as difficult. Complaints systems and rights of redress are important elements of public services (Deakin and Wright 1990; National Consumer Council 1986). Are they part of service quality?

Let us start by looking at whether common characteristics and dimensions of service quality can be catalogued.

The characteristics and dimensions of service quality

Avedis Donabedian (1980, 1982, 1985) devoted many years to defining and measuring quality in medical care. While acknowledging – and documenting in great detail in his three massive volumes on the subject – the different perceptions of patients, doctors and nurses in a variety of clinical situations, he tried to narrow down the definition of quality to a point of manageability and generality that could then be expanded for different situations, at the level of individual patient or of a clinic or hospital as a whole.

He saw some attributes, such as accessibility, continuity and co-ordination, as factors *contributing* to the attainment of quality, while others were seen as *characteristics* of quality itself. Then, within the intrinsic characteristics of quality, Donabedian's analysis identified three broad dimensions of quality. These were:

- The technical dimension: the application of science and technology to a problem.
- The 'non-technical' dimension: the social/psychological interaction between practitioner and client.
- The amenities, or settings of the service.

Donabedian felt that, in a medical setting, these three attributes, or dimensions, of quality were interdependent: the first two were particularly important, but the effect of the local environment on the overall quality had to be acknowledged. He asked himself whether there was a division between people who want the technically best person, without it mattering whether they took a personal interest; and those who want the technician to have the 'best' personal interest. He concluded that both were needed: in a medical setting, the technical efficacy of a service is directly affected by how it is delivered, while the environment – the layout of a ward, its cleanliness, the arrangement of visiting times and possibilities for privacy – can all contribute to a quicker or slower recovery (including, one would guess, the possibility that the environment is so awful that patients discharge themselves too soon, or do not return for follow-up treatment).

Before analysing a little more closely what might be included under each of these three headings, let us see if they are generalizable to other services.

John Stewart and Kieron Walsh (1989) proposed that the quality of a local government service should reflect both whether (or how far) it satisfies users' requirements and whether (how far) it met the public purposes for which it was designed. They note that users' requirements may vary and be in competition with each other and that some services may never meet users' requirements because they exist to meet public (i.e. collective citizens') purposes expressed through legislation and election manifestos.

But in order to assess either the levels of satisfaction or the extent to which public purposes have been met, Stewart and Walsh, like Donabedian, felt that there were three dimensions for analysing the quality of individual services. Couched in slightly different language, they boil down to much the same as those suggested by Donabedian. They are:

- The *core service*: does the service do what it is designed to do, does it meet the requirements of those for whom it is designed?

- The *service surroundings*: is the service supported and enhanced by its surroundings, or local environment?
- The *service relationship*: does the relationship between those providing the service and those receiving it enhance the experience of the core service?

In practice, as these authors and Donabedian acknowledge, it is not always possible to differentiate between the 'service relationship' and the 'core service'. The simple reason is that in services where a large part of the service consists of interaction between provider and consumer – this goes particularly for personal care services – then the relationship *is* the core service. This does not detract from the idea that, when considering quality, one should be thinking about:

- What is the service?
- How is it delivered?
- Does the ambience – the setting – in which the service is delivered enhance or detract from the overall quality of the service?

Technical quality

The idea behind technical quality is that the service does what it is supposed to do. This is sometimes known as 'fitness for purpose', 'fitness for use' or 'conformance to specification'. There are, I think, slight differences between these concepts.

'Conformance to specification' is an approach based on standardization, as in the statistical process control beloved of quality gurus such as Deming (1986) and Crosby (1986). It is an important ingredient for quality control management. It seems to imply a scientific objectivity that may exist for manufactured products but is hardly possible for most services. This is because even the most tightly drawn contract for services has to leave some room for discretion. Individuals are not machines, and delivering services requires a judgement, there is often no clear 'right' or 'wrong'. It is not obvious how to detect a 'defect' or 'variance', essential to the notion of control. Even where procedures are laid down, they must in practice be a guide to action, providing an important set of basic rules but needing also to allow for individual circumstances.

Specifications are often assumed to be producer-driven, but there is no logical reason why, for public services, consumers and others should not be involved in the development of specifications, as they already are in Bradford and Harlow Councils: through their neighbourhood co-ordinator, local citizens have been able to get their needs incorporated into council-wide contract specifications.

'Fitness for use' is a phrase favoured by the quality guru Joseph Juran (1979). It has a rather 'take it or leave it' feel. If the service is usable, that is quality: it is too bad if it does not happen to meet needs or satisfy wants.

'Fitness for purpose' seems to me to be nearer to the kind of quality I am discussing in this book. It carries with it an idea that the purpose of a service, its objectives and underlying values, need to be clearly defined: what is it *for*, as well as what does it *do* or how is it *used*? This phrase does not itself automatically suggest who should be defining that purpose, but we are drawn away from the apparent exclusivity – and 'objectivity' – of the producer. It provides more of an opening for others to be involved.

The technical characteristics of a service designed to increase its fitness for purpose are not necessarily limited to the tangible. This would be very difficult for many services, where much of what is done is intangible and hard to observe (Propper 1992). The actual process of a therapeutic service may be more or less unobservable, the effects even more so. Technical characteristics may have to be defined purely on the basis of professional standards, which are hard for the outsider to judge and are often closely protected by the members of that profession.

Despite such protectionism, professional services – even the most complex of observable or unobservable procedures – *can* be questioned by consumers and citizens, and by colleagues. In some cases – medical and educational services are obvious examples – a second opinion can be sought to verify or check advice and procedures. In others, such as building repairs or environmental planning, it is often possible to find local people who are themselves experienced in the same area of work, who at least know the right questions to ask. Neighbourhood forums, planning consultation meetings and area committees with public question times are all channels for input from detached experts. Similarly, advocacy services representing Asian women patients kept maternity staff on their toes in Hackney, resented at first, then seen as useful partners in service improvement (Winkler 1987).

Technical quality characteristics can apply to any part of a quality service, or to the overall design of the service. One of the ideas behind 'total quality' is that all aspects both of the processes of production and of the outputs to the consumer have to be included. Certainly, in a perfect organization, each part of the process and the links between them ought to reach a high technical quality. As part of the production chain, inputs (the raw ingredients – food, recipes, kitchens), throughputs (technical knowledge and experience – cooks and waitresses/waiters) are all crucial to the outputs (a meal in a restaurant or café). There is more to the success of a good meal than technical expertise and good quality ingredients, but it is unlikely that you would be happy without them.

The public sector has long been characterized by large, complex organizations. Even after purchaser/provider splits, they are still large, while the complexities are even greater. Inputs, throughputs and outputs need to be linked through a process of service design: technical quality needs to cover each of these stages.

Defining the technical quality is not always easy. When I started asking about this, in Birmingham's neighbourhood offices in 1989 (Gaster 1991b), it turned out not to be a simple matter of splitting the service down into identifiable tasks. What were the *purposes* the neighbourhood office service was intended to serve, *who* was it for? It can be very difficult to answer these questions, especially where underlying values are unclear or muddled, where strategic objectives have not been defined and where the needs of both internal and external consumers have to be understood and weighed up.

Nor is it a matter of defining the ideal service. In all services, in the private sector as well as the public, it is rarely a matter of producing a perfect or a luxury service. The aim has to be find the 'best fit' – or 'good enough' as some would say. A whole range of factors need to be fitted together and traded off against each other, within resources, capabilities and the known requirements of public and consumers (Burningham 1992).

Non-technical quality

Non-technical quality – the service relationship, the social/psychological interaction between producer and consumer – is a key, possibly *the* key, to the technical quality actually achieved. The visible, most obvious aspect of non-technical quality is the relationship with the external consumer – the customer, patient, client or community. However, because most services involve several different but linked stages, relationships between internal producers and consumers need to be considered too. The quality of the formal and informal relationships between colleagues, teams and departments (the internal customer) can have very positive or very negative effects on the quality of the service as a whole.

For the direct relationship between organization and consumer, we can turn to the analyses of 'service encounters' by Czepiel *et al.* (1985). The authors examine the nature of the interaction between producer and external consumer in some detail. They also consider process design and relationships between the 'front line' and the 'back line'. The back line is the part of the organization that the external consumer does not see. In a contract relationship, it includes the contractor organizations.

Front-line encounters with the public are often of very high quality. The constraints often come from the failure to support the front line because of poor relationships with the back line and other organizations. In our study of social services and health service relationships in the field of community care we found that these links and relationships are crucial (Smith *et al.* 1993). Many public sector services are in the future going to be delivered not through traditional hierarchical and departmental networks but through effective co-operation between different organizations (Audit Commission 1993b). These will each be driven by their own values and objectives. How these can best be harnessed and matched for the benefit of services as a whole now constitutes an important element in non-technical quality. Integrationist values, the ability to work across organizational boundaries, will be bedrock requirements for the 1990s and beyond.

Characteristics of non-technical quality

Studies of various services reveal some key elements of service encounters. Thus, from the service user's point of view, the five top qualities for social security (Heald and Stodel 1988) were:

1 Helpful staff.
2 Knowledgeable staff.
3 Not to be overheard (privacy).
4 Staff have time for you.
5 You can ask questions.

In Birmingham neighbourhood offices staff perceptions varied. However, all front-line staff – generic neighbourhood office staff, housing staff and social service staff – saw accessibility as a key requirement (Gaster 1990). Other quality characteristics included:

• Listening, giving time, empathizing, thinking through, giving enough information for options to be clear, not 'fobbing off', sensitivity to individual needs, fairness, honesty, treating people equally, being polite, friendly and ensuring a speedy response (Neighbourhood Office staff).
• Being open with people, providing full information, looking at alternative possibilities, minimum waiting, sensitive, trustworthy, responsive staff – and speedy response (Housing staff).
• Understanding, being knowledgeable, flexibility, equal treatment and 'do as you would be done by', minimum waiting, offering real choice, consumer involvement (Social Services staff).

It was striking in the Birmingham research that staff distinguished between two aspects of non-technical quality. Some aspects they felt were within their own control: these could be improved through better internal procedures and appropriate training. In contrast, some key elements were not within their power, most prominent of which were 'speedy response' and 'offering real choice'. These both depended on the co-operation and support of other departments or sections within the Council – the back line.

Finally, a survey of four housing departments by the Institute of Local Government Studies (1989) asked tenants to rate not only what they were looking for in a housing office, but also how good the offices were in practice. This showed wide discrepancies between requirements and practice. Staff who 'understand' and who 'explain' were seen as the top priorities, but, like the desire for privacy, they came low on the list of the councils' actual perceived practice. Friendly staff were desirable (and often existed), but 'continuity', that is, being seen by the same person, the fourth most important characteristic, came very low indeed on the list of what tenants actually experienced.

Customer care training is, in essence, directed towards ensuring consistency of treatment in this area of non-technical quality. This training, which will be discussed in detail when considering implementation programmes for quality, may well help staff to be more aware of what needs to be done to improve their own interactions with the public. If, however, it does not address the customer care provided by the whole organization, and focuses purely on front-line staff, it does only half the job. Are these staff simply being trained 'how to say "no" nicely'?

Communication

Underlying many of the non-technical characteristics of quality and, for personal services, the technical quality too, is the need to be able to communicate well. It is extraordinary how little attention seems to be paid to this important factor, either in the training of many professionals or for the administrative and reception staff who are so often the first people the public comes into contact with. Yet 'first impressions' (the original title of Jane Austen's *Pride and prejudice*) can also be lasting impressions. Insensitive or unintelligible reactions at the first encounter can take a long time to undo. And how many organizational analyses have identified poor internal communication as the key problem in implementing new policies, including quality policies?

Communication can be face-to-face, on the telephone or in correspondence. Non-verbal communication is as important as verbal communication. Few front-line staff, for example, are aware of the effect of body language or tone of voice on the quality of the encounter (Nyquist *et al.* 1985). And verbal communication needs to be backed up by other methods, often in written form (including translations, braille and large print where relevant and affordable).

A survey by the Centre for Health Economics (1991b) underlined the need for high quality information as part of medical treatment. This research gives some useful pointers to other services. For example they quote P. Ley's findings that patients had forgotten half the information they were given five minutes after the end of an outpatient visit. Suggested reasons for this were:

- High levels of anxiety and frustration, particularly after long waiting periods.
- Inhibition from asking questions because of social distance between doctor and patient.
- Inability to understand medical jargon.

Better communication can be a form of empowerment, where the consumer – the patient and family in this case – can understand and make real choices. However, it may be less about giving patients a say, more about ensuring that patients do what the doctors tell them! Patients would be able to 'comply' better:

> The research findings support the belief that providing clinical information to patients does have a beneficial effect on the outcome of treatment in that patients are more likely to retain information and comply with treatment programmes if information is given in written form.
>
> (Centre for Health Economics 1991b: 2)

While one might wish to question the professional/producer-led values that appear to underlie this statement, the research also included a critical review of hospital leaflets and pamphlets by a panel of ex-patients. They looked at the presentation, content, style and attitudes such as sympathy and empathy represented within the written material. These official leaflets were found to present images and language that were often didactic and that failed to understand or relate to different social and ethnic backgrounds; they were generally slanted towards the Caucasian English-speaking nuclear family. The panel compared these leaflets with some prepared by voluntary and self-help groups. These were generally found to be more user-friendly. Unfortunately, they could also go out of date quickly if funds were not available for updating them.

Low quality communication in public services is not confined to relationships between individuals. In public meetings or in other forums, officers, councillors or Board members may appear to be defensive, seeing questions and comments as a form of criticism. Bureaucratic language and rigid agendas, formal seating arrangements where the officers dominate and the public has to squeeze in, can all lead local groups and members of the public to feel cynical and alienated. A mature dialogue and a joint approach to problem solving and quality improvement is then very difficult to achieve.

Quality in the service setting

Just as 'non-technical' qualities can strengthen or weaken the chances of delivering a high quality 'technical' service, so the service setting can enhance or undermine the rest of the service. It is particularly relevant to the front line. It is from the experience of this part of the organization, the boundary with the outside world, that the rest of the organization will be judged. What message is being given to people encountering the organization for the first (or the 100th) time?

Front-line staff may not have much control over their environment. It may, indeed, be a source of frustration to them. The management of buildings, their design and decoration, is often controlled by staff uninvolved in the day-to-day service. Redecoration and comfortable chairs might be desirable, but they may be seen as self-indulgent, a low priority.

On the other hand, physical barriers often exist because staff have asked for them – in local authority housing or social service offices, for example. Signposting may be minimal because there is no real desire to welcome people in. Queuing and waiting arrangements may be confused and alienating because the receptionist is the least valued person in the organization and no-one else is prepared, having perhaps 'risen above' such activities themselves, to give much thought or support to what is going on before consumers reach their part of the service. If one works in a building day after day, one can get so used to it that one loses sensitivity to the effect of the 'grot' on the anxious citizen seeking help.

Richard E. Wener (1985) identified three levels of what he called the 'environmental psychology' of services. Although he, like all the contributors to Czepiel *et al.*'s book, was talking about the private sector, this is one area where there is transferability of ideas between private and other sectors. The three levels were:

1 The *ergonomics*: heat, light, warmth, noise, furniture design. Quite simply, are callers made comfortable?
2 The *social ecology*: is there enough privacy, are people crowded together – or are they possibly too distant from each other (behind a desk, on a platform)?
3 The *meaning*: what are the messages being given as to the behaviour to be expected. Do the staff fear you – or are you supposed to fear them? Are you socially desirable – or not? How are the staff themselves expected to behave? Is the situation under control or is there too much stress present?

Environments do influence how people feel and how they behave. A bad environmental setting can produce consumers who are angry, fearful or disoriented; in the same setting service providers can be defensive, frustrated and disorganized. None of this is likely to lead to a high quality service. An unwelcoming setting, especially for a service that people do not necessarily want and may feel stigmatized in using (social services, prisons) will lead to low-level service encounters, where constructive listening and dialogue are impossible and contact is kept to the basic minimum.

Improving the quality of the service setting is not technically difficult. Some aspects, like the need for security and, at the same time, the desire for open access, may appear to conflict with each other. Trade-offs – building up some aspects of security by installing alarms, working out mutually supportive safety procedures while ensuring that staff can be seen and are approachable – can offset the needs and anxieties of staff against the needs and anxieties of consumers. However, although plants, paint and name badges can be introduced, they may appear tokenistic if they are not linked to a broader policy for quality.

What is the message the organization wants to put across, to its staff and to its consumers, about how they are valued? How does that relate to the local community? Is it a sign of respect to build a glossy office in the middle of a run-down housing estate, or is it kicking local people in the teeth, making a statement about the relative worth of employees and tenants? If junior staff, perhaps vulnerable to harassment, wear (legible) name badges but senior staff do not, what does that say about how front-line staff are valued within the organization?

Combining the different dimensions of quality

A good environment and good non-technical quality can make the technical quality better, more effective. They are not substitutes for it. High levels of technical quality, where workers know what they are meant to be doing and do it to the best of their ability, are essential to the quality of public services. However, in all public services, the need for understanding, respect, explanation and, where possible, choice, puts a high premium on the interpersonal qualities of the service, especially where rationing, resource constraints, government policies and the national economy limit the services that can in practice be provided.

It seems to me the quality characteristics of most services can be contained within the three dimensions described in the last few pages. There would certainly be some debate about where certain attributes come – is reliability a technical or a non-technical characteristic? The great advantage of the three-dimensional approach is that it becomes possible to think clearly about each individual service. Starting with frameworks of service and organizational objectives, and taking into account the range of values that the organization explicitly or by implication embraces, the detailed characteristics of each service can be defined pragmatically along technical, non-technical and environmental dimensions.

Satisfaction scores

So far, we have looked at quality as though it were an objective fact that could be dissected, analysed and brought together in neat, measurable packages. This does not tell us what we are actually aiming to achieve. Identifying the dimensions and characteristics could lead to high quality. It could also lead to low or 'good enough' quality.

Something else is needed to bring a focus, to help determine the standards being aimed for, and to provide a basis for measurement. Can the concept of 'satisfaction' help? If a service is satisfactory, does this mean that, as perceived by those with an interest (not solely the consumer), it is of high quality?

Instinctively, there is a close relationship between satisfaction and quality. For private sector services, this seemed to be confirmed by research by Parasuraman, Zeithaml and Berry in the mid-1980s: if we are satisfied, the service must have been of high quality. According to this scenario, all that has to be done is to satisfy consumers, and quality is assured. There are, however, quite a lot of problems with this idea, especially as it applies to the public services. Let us start with three.

First, what satisfies me will not necessarily satisfy you, because I might not have been looking for the same things from the service. Robert Pirsig (1974) distinguished emotional quality, reflecting current feelings and immediate reactions, from a more rational approach, which he called intellectual or classical quality: satisfaction is determined after taking into account a host of relevant factors, including projected outcomes. Even so, the differences between people's assessment of satisfaction will still be wide, because of their different starting points.

For this reason, the idea that quality can be measured through satisfaction scores has a limited value. If everyone who is asked has a different notion of what will be satisfactory to them, how can the results be used to identify service improvements? It is necessary to look more deeply at what constitutes satisfaction or dissatisfaction.

Third, do public services all have as one of their purposes the requirement to provide satisfaction? Is there, perhaps, a danger of seeking popularity and lack of hassle at the cost of some of the other purposes and values? Are probation officers paid to be popular?

Two examples of this dilemma come to mind. The first is an example rather close to home, the evaluation of teaching. Should a favourable set of students' comments about a course of lectures give the lecturer a sense of complacency and well-being? Or might it mean that the course was not challenging enough – or that perhaps the friendly, humorous manner in which it was delivered obscured the fact that the content could have been better prepared? High levels of stated satisfaction might be good for the lecturer's career progression, as the comments work their way into the university's records. They might be less good for next year's students, as there was no incentive for the lectures to be improved.

If the aim of a service is to satisfy the majority (satisfaction scores measure this) how are minority rights and concerns to be protected? Public housing allocations are now routinely monitored for the ethnic origin of the applicant because of findings of widespread racial discrimination in several housing departments in the late 1970s and early 1980s. A satisfaction survey of tenants living in 'nice' estates – those without black tenants or single parents, unemployed or other 'undesirable' categories – would undoubtedly have shown 'net satisfaction' (as MORI measures it – that is, the number satisfied minus the number dissatisfied). Relying on satisfaction scores would bring the bizarre result that a discriminatory service is a high quality service.

These two examples show both the pitfalls of simplistic measurement and performance indicators (to be examined in Chapter 6) and the significance of values, particularly the protection of minority rights, as buffers against populism and going for the easy option.

Satisfaction and expectations: the Parasuraman–Zeithaml–Berry 'gaps' model of quality

If you expect little or nothing – the experience of many public sector clients – then the simple fact of being listened to can produce rapturous satisfaction scores. Conversely, if you have high expectations – perhaps because of publicity hype, or because someone you know was well treated – disappointment with the actual experience of the service can result in low levels of satisfaction. There is, in other words, a strong relationship between expectations and satisfaction. Expectations are formed from both perceptions and direct experience (Maister 1985). Maister observes that both expectations and perceptions are psychological phenomena. This needs to be understood by service providers (all of whom are, in other parts of their lives, service consumers). Action can be taken, not so much to manipulate people to feel satisfied (though that is a danger), but to close the gap between expectations and experience.

The Parasuraman–Zeithaml–Berry explanation of service quality (Parasuraman et al. 1988a) identified key gaps, or discrepancies, in the organization of services that would affect their ultimate quality. Because services are, as they point out, intangible, heterogeneous and largely inseparable from the client (the client affects the service and is part of it), attitudes, expectations and perceptions are all crucial both to the final outcome and to the process of service delivery. These attitudes, perceptions and expectations are formed in many different ways, and affect both consumers and, at a series of stages, the service producers. At each stage, there may be a gap between the expectations, perceptions and the ability to deliver the right service.

Using focus groups, they established that for a range of private services (retail banking, securities brokerage, appliance repair and maintenance, credit cards) satisfaction was essential to quality:

> The focus groups unambiguously supported the notion that the key to good service quality is meeting or exceeding what customers expect from the service.
>
> (Parasuraman *et al.* 1988a: 46)

It is important to be cautious here. These writers did not, apparently, consider the possibility of low expectations leading to easy satisfaction, nor did they consider whether satisfaction is an appropriate concept for services that people might not want or have chosen to receive – or that they want but cannot have. However, the model is useful in identifying where the gaps lie. Three common mismatches are:

1 Consumer expectations versus management perceptions of what the service should be.
2 Actual service delivery versus information about the service.
3 Expected service versus perceived service.

The 'we know best' attitude is clearly reflected in the first gap, while the second is a useful reminder either that there is often little information available or that, in some cases, publicity has gone ahead of the fact: expectations were raised too high.

The third gap raises more profound issues of where expectations and perceptions are coming from. How are expectations formed, what are the factors that mould them?

How are expectations formed?

All services have to some extent to be taken on trust. They cannot, unlike manufactured goods, be stored and inspected before they are consumed. However, some services are frequently or continuously used by individuals and their families, while some may amount to a single episode in a person's life. To the service producer (doctor, social worker, housing adviser or job trainer), for whom the service is a daily routine, these differences may not be apparent. Procedures, routines and, sometimes, the cutting of corners for the convenience of the producer can lead to insensitivity and unintended adverse effects on the consumer.

Frequency and length of use, then, are factors that will affect expectations. The more often – or the longer – a service is used, the smaller will be the gap between what people expect and what they actually get. This does not in itself define satisfaction, of course. Expectations, even those based on know-ledge and experience of the service, may still be low: the service may be historically of poor quality (does not meet its specification), or consumers may have low self-esteem.

Second, services affect consumers in different ways. A house repair is very different from an operation for cancer, just as failure of rubbish collection is different from being homeless. Anxieties, hopes, fears and expectations will be very different, in proportion to the service's significance to the overall quality of life of individuals or communities.

Third, expectations are influenced by how much both producers and consumers know, about what is needed and about what can be offered respec-tively. Knowledge relates partly to familiarity with the service. Frequent or continuous use can help a consumer guess what to expect next time. Unfor-tunately, in a service culture where on the whole consumers have had to fit in with the service has on offer, rather than services fitting the needs of consumers and citizens, that experience might not take you very far. There is still a problem of finding out what you don't know.

Social service departments now have to analyse local community care needs, both as the basis for care management and for developing local 'markets' of providers to meet local purchasing requirements. If, despite their often expressed fear of 'raising expectations', they also begin to inform residents about their rights and choice of service, good quality mutual knowledge could bridge a gap between the expectations of consumers and providers alike.

A fourth ingredient in the formation of expectations is attitudes. A pre-vious bad experience can lead to an expectation or a fear that similar treatment will be meted out next time. So the service user can approach the next service episode more grudgingly, more fearfully, or with lower expectations. Prejudice also affects attitudes: it means that people are not treated according to their needs, or listened to because of their knowledge and skills, but are slotted into some general stereotype.

Finally, feelings are important. Services are often sought at a time of maximum vulnerability. This affects both expectations and perceptions: you may expect little, be unable to assert what rights you have, but are dispropor-tionately grateful if anything is done at all. It is only after the service has been received, when you have left hospital or had your home repaired, that the sense of powerlessness and dependence can be shed. For this reason, advocates may be useful in the process of service implementation. In service planning and monitoring, groups can be far more powerful than individuals. 'Survivors' can speak out for those who are still in the process of receiving the service.

Who should define public service quality? Negotiations and trade-offs

The private sector is realizing that knowledge of customer needs is essential for quality. Here, where the aim is to improve competitive edge, the matter is seen as the relatively simple one of 'meeting customers' requirements' (Oakland 1989) and maximizing customer satisfaction.

In the public sector, which is paid for by, and has duties to, the wider community, and where 'customers' cannot normally take their custom elsewhere, the picture is far more complicated. It is not simply a matter of meeting expressed needs, but of finding out unexpressed needs, setting priorities, allocating resources and publicly justifying and accounting for what has been done.

The previous chapter analysed the array of 'interests' involved in public services. The idea that quality definitions should be *negotiated* becomes self-evident. It is all the more important because different expectations and perceptions affect the very survival of public services. If they are not known or valued, no-one will defend them.

Once the idea of negotiation is introduced, and that of objective, scientific quality rejected, it becomes clear that part of the negotiation must relate to what goes into definitions of quality and what does not. How are legal, financial, political constraints incorporated, and how are core values reflected? In addition, desirable characteristics, as perceived by the different parties to the negotiation, will probably have to be balanced against each other: waiting times might be 'traded off' against listening time and thoroughness; the desires of the majority balanced with the needs of the minority; the need to protect society may override the freedom of the individual. A GP group practice in Islington was recently praised by the Audit Commission for saving prescription costs because its policy was to spend more time with patients, finding out their real needs; at the same time, they were failing to meet Government throughput targets. They were surprised to be praised for what they thought was normal practice (*The Guardian* 8 March 1994).

These are not new conflicts, in fact some, especially those relating to freedom and equality, are very old ones. However, incorporating them into the debate about what constitutes the quality of a service makes explicit the fact that not all needs can be satisfied. It also makes explicit the actual nature of the service, including its non-technical characteristics and its 'service setting'. It is a process that could make the real priorities of each party to the negotiation uncomfortably clear, but could also lead to honest and clear agreements, and a sense of ownership of the result. Ownership cannot guarantee that a policy will be successfully implemented, but the overwhelming consensus among quality gurus and writers on organizational change is that implementation is seriously impeded if commitment and understanding have not been sought.

Negotiating the definition of quality in contracts

Much has been written about the advantages and disadvantages of the contract process in public services. This is not the place to enter that debate. The fact is that many public services are now being delivered or are about to be delivered through a contractual process. The question for us is how this affects the processes of negotiation between interested parties.

Kieron Walsh (1993) has written of the dangers of contracts that define everything to the minutest detail. Overspecification leaves very little room for the flexibility and sensitivity needed in so many public services. It also leads to an increasing array of statistical returns, putting huge pressure on provider organizations. The quality of their work, especially those in the voluntary sector with minimal administrative back-up, may suffer in the process.

Then, partly because those in the public services are relatively new to the game, contract negotiation is being seen as a highly technical process. This has the effect of excluding users or citizens. It is rare for front-line managers to get involved, except in some of the decentralized and devolved agencies such as Devon Social Services, or Southwark Housing Department.

Some public involvement in contract specification is now beginning to be possible, building on local consultation infrastructures. However, depending on the duration of contracts, opportunities for such involvement are likely to be limited, as they may only take place every few years. An additional limitation is that contracts tend to focus on the fitness for purpose dimension of quality, giving relatively little attention to the non-technical and environmental aspects of a service.

Where the contract is flexible enough to allow such discussion, negotiation of these aspects of service ought to be possible after the contract is in place: the details of how and where the service is to be delivered could well be the subject of discussion between users, local residents and the service provider. Providers will certainly want some feedback from users, they may also want some ideas of what service is most acceptable and satisfactory – how closely, in other words, expectations match perceptions and experience. This will help in future contract bids. An incentive exists for providers to encourage involvement – and the Newcastle example of involvement of a mental health users' group shows what can happen in practice (Harrison 1993).

In principle, then, the definition of quality could be negotiated with users and citizens by both purchaser and provider. In practice, there are some obvious difficulties, not least the possibility of participation fatigue, where voluntary and community groups are constantly being requested to send a representative to every working party in sight. The time and cost of participation is a real problem for any organization involved in it. It is far greater for those with few resources, dependent on volunteers or a few precariously paid staff (Martin and Gaster 1993).

Connecting definitions with organizational values

Equality, equity and quality

Equality is a value that has to suffuse every action of the organization if it is to be meaningful and credible. In the public sector, and in public services, quality and equality are closely, some would say inextricably linked.

Improving service quality and equal opportunities are strongly inter-related. Improving quality requires the authority to treat each customer as an individual, but also to recognise the specific needs and experiences that come with their membership of a particular group. Similarly, the development of equal opportunities involves an awareness of those barriers which obstruct the relationship between groups in the community and the organisation.

(Local Government Management Board 1991: 1)

In the 1980s, when equal opportunities were on the agenda of many public authorities, there was little talk of quality. Once equal opportunities began to move from the internal realm of recruitment and promotion to the external policies of service delivery, the idea began to gain ground that services would be better (i.e. the quality would improve) if they were delivered fairly to all members of the community. While this might involve geographical or social targeting and take-up campaigns, it could also involve changing the internal ways of working – the culture – to ensure awareness of equality issues and to prevent discrimination. Non-discriminatory behaviour then becomes a *de facto* part of the *non-technical* quality, the service relationship, covering access to services and the way that services are delivered.

However, while one might argue that they *should* include equality characteristics, there is no guarantee that quality definitions *will* do so: this depends on the organizational values and attitudes.

Equity is about making sure that services are fairly distributed. Many would argue that this is what defines public services, making them different from private or voluntary ones. A service organization with equity as one of its values would demonstrate this through, for example, defining within the *technical* quality the need to monitor and evaluate who has actually received the service. If it was found that no-one on a particular estate used the housing benefit services, or if it was only the middle classes that were getting routine operations in hospitals, a high quality service would be trying to find out why.

Value for money

I have argued elsewhere (Gaster 1992c) that economy and efficiency are not part of the definition of quality. Policies designed to improve value for money will not necessarily enhance quality. They may help managers develop and control budgets in line with actual needs, and to develop more responsive services, but they could also detract from quality. If priority is given to throughput, as is already happening in the Hospital Trusts, the rapid discharge of patients emphasizes standardization and speed over flexibility, co-ordination and sensitivity. There is no neat and tidy relationship between value for money and quality. A good quality service needs to be efficient, but an efficient service may not be meeting agreed needs, one of the tests of quality.

Conclusion

Defining quality in public services is no easy matter. Services are not like manufactured goods, where quality processes and definitions are relatively straightforward. They involve individual transactions which, whatever the attempts to standardize them ('Have a nice day . . .') will, except in the most routine of services, each be different. Not only that, but the essence of quality in services, and especially the public services, is that these differences are an inherent part of the service itself: it is appropriate responses to *different* needs that are needed. Criticisms of public services in the past have centred on the treatment of individuals as though they were machine parts on a conveyor belt.

So services are different from goods, and public services are different from private services. The relationship of public services, not only with direct consumers but with the whole community to which they are ultimately accountable, makes them different from private services, where profit and market share (and accountability to shareholders) are the driving forces.

Definitions of public service quality has to take account of these differences. Taking ideas both from other writers on both public and private services and from my own research, I have pursued four points in this and the previous chapter:

1 The dimensions of quality can be defined in three ways: the technical (what?) dimension, the non-technical (how?) dimension and the environmental (where?) dimension. I have suggested that most characteristics of quality can be analysed along these dimensions, which apply to the whole process of service production, from inputs to outcomes.
2 The idea that quality is closely related to satisfaction is useful but has its limitations. The recognition that there is often a gap between expectations and perceptions or experience is, however, important to the way that the three dimensions of quality are constructed, interpreted and, eventually, implemented.
3 Partly to bridge that gap and partly because of the nature of public services, where there are few opportunities to choose to go elsewhere, there is a need for dialogue and negotiation between the main parties to service production and consumption. This includes not only immediate consumers, but also the wider community. It exposes the need for trade-offs between quality characteristics, as well as the differences between ideal and realistic quality standards. The decision-making role of the public service organization, especially as client or purchaser, needs to be acknowledged, but I suggest that decisions about how service quality is defined will have greater legitimacy, ownership and commitment if they are democratic and participative.
4 While there are no hard and fast boundaries between the quality of a service and other characteristics such as fairness, efficiency or cost, I suggest that these factors are separable from the notion of quality. This is partly to avoid the definition of quality from becoming hopelessly wide and partly because, while such characteristics can be complementary and in some cases mutually

dependent, they can and do exist without each other, being based on different values, generating different policies, and requiring different programmes of action.

Public service managers face a whole range of dilemmas and contradictions when trying to improve the quality of their services, not least because of the economic and political climate in which they now have to survive. They need to be clearer than ever about the nature of their service, about the quality characteristics that need to be improved or conserved, and about the public sector values and objectives that inform the negotiations about what is important.

This is a route not only to making the services better, but to making them more accountable and more widely supported. It is important to be optimistic about the future of public services. The framework suggested in this chapter could help to preserve public service managers from becoming the victims of overzealous and legalistic contract officers. It could help them assess the relevance of quality consultants with briefcases full of 'how to' recipes. And it could support them in resisting articulate consumers, remote central managers or financial and performance managers bringing undue pressure at the expense of other less powerful groups in society. It is all about being clear what you are doing, why you are doing it, being able to demonstrate that you are doing it, and ensuring that you are supported in doing so.

However, there are some practical considerations to what otherwise sounds like yet another set of missionary ideas. How does it all get done? Policies and definitions are all very well, but can they be put into practice? The next two chapters look at these questions.

4

Principles of implementation

Setting the scene

This and the next chapter are about managing quality. They are not a set of recipes for 'doing' quality, but an attempt to analyse existing models and to provide a framework for public service managers to think about implementing quality policies in their own services. They take us from the stage in Figure 1.1 where values, strategic objectives and definitions have been tackled, moving on to the phases of diagnosis and implementation.

There are plenty of 'how to' books on the market, and managers can, if they choose, pick one off the station or airport bookstalls and get on with it. However, when they are opened, it will be found that most of these books apply to the private sector, and very often to the manufacturing sector. They are therefore largely concerned with market share and profitability, with the production of goods and services that the public wants or can be persuaded to want. Also, even in the small batch production methods of the post-Fordist era (if it is really here), their main aim is to standardize and reduce variance to the point, sometimes, of zero defects. However, service interactions cannot and should not be standardized in the same way that manufactured products can. Public services carry out public purposes, balancing the needs and wants of different groups in society, including the least powerful. They are accountable for public monies and aiming not just to meet individual needs, but to improve the quality of life for the whole community.

A problem affecting the whole of the quality debate is the lack of detailed research into whether quality systems, once introduced, do or do not improve the actual quality of the service. In the public services, research has tended either to test users' opinions, without relating that to service production systems; or to count and sometimes analyse management systems and structures, without relating them to the service produced. It is equally difficult in the private sector to find evidence of the effect of a quality programme on outputs and outcomes. Peters and Waterman (1982) analysed the characteristics of 'excellent' (i.e. continuously innovative and long-term profitable) companies, but their research was more a process of induction than of investigating planned quality programmes in relation to performance. Other gurus scarcely mention the notion of systematic research. The sources for their models are their own ideas and experience, which relate almost exclusively to management processes. Outcomes are assumed but not tested.

Lacking a solid research base, I set out in this chapter to develop a set of *criteria* for judging the appropriateness and relevance of different quality systems to the needs of public services. My own preferences will no doubt emerge, particularly for a systematic approach based on rational analysis, but I hope that what I have to offer will be helpful on a broader front, enabling public service managers to make their own judgments about the system that best suits their present needs and future aims.

Before introducing these criteria in the form of a checklist at the end of the chapter, I shall examine what I see as a key component in the quality management process: the 'service', or 'quality chain'. This will underline the need for attention to detail at every stage of delivering a service. Mapping and understanding the component parts of a service and the connections between each link gives the starting point for a process of diagnosing the service as a whole. From this diagnosis, options for action can be generated. Diagnosis and action planning are probably the core of quality management systems.

Then I look at ways of mapping existing quality systems, using the Audit Commission's 'quality map' and an approach developed at the Centre for Health Economics at York University. These show how existing quality systems generally cover only part of the whole.

In Chapter 5, some of the main systems − quality control, quality assurance, total quality management and customer care − will be examined, checked against the criteria suggested in this chapter and located on the quality map. Does each of these systems have a clear definition? Are they understood in the same way by all who use them, or are they subject to a wide variety of interpretations? I shall also look at diagnostic techniques, organizational structures and, finally, the most important issue of all, organizational cultures.

Quality chains and service gaps

Departments and sections of public sector organizations often behave as if they were independent entities, with little connection (except under duress) with other departments. This attitude, common to many parts of the public sector though not confined to it, is − must be − detrimental to the aim of improving service quality. Almost all services depend in one way or another on other services, as part of the input, throughput or output, and sometimes all three.

The quality or service chain is therefore a key piece of the jigsaw of quality. It is both a diagnostic tool, and the basis for a programme of action. It highlights not only the interdependence of a great many apparently separate actions, but also the fact that for each stage of a service process, there is a producer and a consumer. If quality is about service to the consumer, then this applies as much to the relationships along the chain as it does to the ultimate link, that at the boundary between the organization and the public.

The quality chain is 'the linkage of internal or external support services, all of which must be of high quality if the service to the public is also to be of high quality' (Audit Commission 1993b: 9).

Analysing the chain

A way of finding out how the chain is made up is to use a critical path analysis: the necessary actions to produce a particular result are analysed to see who has to do what, and when, in order to produce the most efficient result. It is a useful technique that clarifies how many different actions make up a complete service, some of which other service providers, themselves links in the chain, may be unaware of. It also clarifies different, often fragmented areas of responsibility.

Some chains may be relatively short. A council tenant may report a broken window, for example. After a visit or phone call to a neighbourhood or housing office, the repair is logged into the system. Then come inspection and analysis of what needs to be done, ordering any supplies, arranging access for the workforce, carrying out the job and possibly post-inspection. Each of these is a link in the service chain.

Even in this relatively short chain plenty of things can go wrong, as those on the front desks in housing and neighbourhood offices testify only too often. Reasons for this will of course vary from place to place, but one of the most important is that the whole process is not under the control of one person or department (even before compulsory competitive tendering (CCT)): the need for good communication, clear procedures and high levels of co-operation between the different links become immediately apparent, as does the need for a variety of technical skills along the way (accurate input of repair details; knowledgeable inspection, including decisions on urgency; management skills for best use of repairs team; carpentry or glazier skills of the workforce).

More complex services, such as medical care, social work or community development, have longer or more complicated chains, and a wider range of relationships with the public, as users (direct and indirect) and local residents. Some services – the production of a Council's annual report to satisfy statutory requirements, for example – can appear to be almost entirely internal: the consumers are thought to be councillors and the district auditor. It is easy to forget that the ultimate consumer is the public, and that the way information is collected and presented can affect service departments, public relations sections and other organizations on whose goodwill the Council depends. An analysis of the service chain can reveal these links.

The chain includes the public

The service chain is an extremely practical notion, relevant to all public services. This is usefully illustrated in a recent study of Dutch public services.

In 1992, the Dutch Ministry of Home Affairs published a study (Humbert *et al.* 1992) which, in the interests of 'improving government service to the public', examined ideas for providing integrated front-desk functions for a full range of government services (including those provided by local government). They called these integrated offices 'government service centres'. Their aim would be to:

- Provide information and advice.
- Supply routine products (e.g. abstracts from births and deaths registers).
- Handle more complex questions such as housing allocation and welfare benefits.

Such offices (often known as one-stop shops, or neighbourhood offices in the UK) would give better access to the public, while reducing overlap between service providers and breaking down compartmentalism. Their costs would be in the administrative and organizational changes needed to make them happen, and in the training required for the new front-line staff. The aim of the study was to help weigh up the relative costs and benefits before going ahead, in the context of a welfare state that, through increased fragmentation and specialization 'is characterised by a complex impenetrable organisational structure' (Humbert *et al.* 1992: 8).

The Dutch study identified several key stages of service, which are helpful in developing the concept of a service or quality chain. These stages, seen from the consumer's point of view, were:

- *Awareness*: consumers need to know their rights and commitments; they need to be aware of what services are available. The government needs to be aware of and knowledgeable about its target group, and to carry out 'promotional activities' to ensure that the right information reaches these groups.
- *Formulation of demand*: the public needs to be able to formulate demand in a way that will be responded to. (And, although this study does not say so, there is the opposite presumption that, where it has the freedom to do so, the Government needs to tailor its offerings to what is demanded.)
- *Interaction*: the demand has to be translated into a programme of action. The contact between the public and the government has to be conducted in such a way as to enhance that process.
- *Service offering*: the right service is provided.

The idea of the service centre is to resolve the 'bottlenecks' that occur during this process. This includes the internal bottlenecks, between front line and back line, and between departments whose co-ordinated activity is needed to provide the full service. The stage of service interaction is the point at which the internal service connections – the chain – has to be identified.

This analysis is a useful reminder that the service chain is not an isolated internal feature: it has to connect with the consumer and with the wider public at both ends, not just in terms of response to specific demands, but as a complete system that takes into account the public purposes for which the service was established in the first place.

Gaps analysis

Saying what the service consists of, which is what the analysis of the service chain is all about, is helpful as a launching pad for the next phase, which is to address the weak links in the chain and to improve the service design. Total quality management enthusiasts will argue that this is exactly what total quality management, covering the activities of the whole organization, is intended to do. In practice, many quality programmes are confined to departments or specialities, which can lead to rather a narrow (and sometimes smug) approach. They start from the premise that 'you have to start somewhere' – and corporate initiatives are hard to get off the ground.

The problem is – as I found in the Birmingham neighbourhood offices – that even if you can identify and make explicit the functional links and the weak points between different parts of an organization (or between separate organizations), if you cannot control the links and if there is no incentive for other departments to co-operate, an isolated approach to quality merely in-creases disappointment and disillusion. Multi-service offices such as these are particularly dependent on other parts of the organization for their effectiveness: but in most organizations, especially those with devolved service units, it would be difficult to find activities that did not in some respect depend on others for their overall delivery.

Within this concept of linkages and weak points in a chain comes the notion of service gaps, developed initially by Parasuraman, Zeithaml and Berry in the mid-1980s and now being developed in the British local government context by Speller and Ghobadian (1993). Consumer satisfaction (see Chapter 3) could be analysed in terms of the gaps between consumer expectations and perceptions. The gap is between producers' and consumers' knowledge, un-derstanding and expectations of service.

Service quality is affected by two further gaps. One is at management level, between the perception of what is required and the ability then to specify what needs to be done. The second is between specification and actual performance.

For our purposes, the utility of the model is: (1) to show that different *sources* of expectations and experience exist within an organization; and (2) to see that in many cases the *actual* expectations and experience do not necessarily coincide. In the worst cases, they can be badly divergent. Speller (1992), testing the model in

Stevenage district council, found a further gap between front-line and senior managers. Senior managers did not know what went on at the front line, and there was poor communication at all levels. My work on decentralized organizations, where the front line is often physically as well as psychologically isolated, shows how common this gap is. The result is that front-line staff do not trust senior management, feeling it to be remote and out of practice. The credibility of top-down policies, however apposite and timely, is inevitably limited as a result.

A further gap might be added. This is the gap between politicians' (or Board members') perceptions of what is required and management solutions. It is a gap caused by lack of clarity on the part of the politicians – perhaps an inability to specify objectives in a way that can be translated into action – and by officer reluctance to change long-standing ways of doing things, perhaps feeling that the politicians do not understand the realities of service delivery or the needs of 'professionalism' and existing codes of practice.

While not all organizations providing public services experience all the gaps highlighted in this analysis, the idea is helpful because it identifies where some of the weak links in the chain may be. It suggests that a systematic analysis of these particular gaps (without, presumably, excluding the possibility that there may be others) could or even should be done for any organization serious about quality. How the analysis is carried out is, of course, important. The gaps need to be bridged. It would not be helpful for them to be widened by mutual blame sessions about technical failures.

If the reasons for the gaps – the weak links in the chain – are differences in perceptions, attitudes and expectations, the solution is less with rules and procedures and more on clarity of goals, commitment to quality and improved communication. Devolving control and discretion to individual workers and teams can in itself improve quality:

> We propose that when employees perceive themselves to be in control of situations they encounter in their jobs, they experience less stress. Lower levels of stress lead . . . to higher performance. When employees perceive that they can act flexibly rather than by rote in problem situations en-countered in providing services, control increases and performance improves.
>
> (Zeithaml *et al.* 1988: 42)

If analysing the service chain and identifying gaps (weak links) within it is one important tool in quality management, another is the existence of a suit-able organizational infrastructure. This provides the foundation for systems to improve quality. Without a solid base the superstructure is likely to be flimsy and vulnerable to the winds and whims of change.

Organizational infrastructures

A public service organization that does not identify some need for quality improvement would have to very sure that, within formal requirements, the services it provided met current and future needs in the most satisfactory way possible. It would have an organizational culture, structure and management ethos, deriving from an explicit value base, that would enable it to respond to change flexibly and appropriately, in policy and practice. It would be clear what its service(s) were intended to achieve. It would have ensured that staff, users and the public were aware of these intentions and that key interest groups supported them (or, if they could not support, had agreed to differ), having been consulted and, where necessary, empowered to take part in the debate. It would recognize that, in the public sector as much as in other sectors of service delivery, there is never a moment when it is possible to say 'we've done it!', because the dynamism of political, social and economic change requires constant responses and new initiatives if the organization wishes to survive.

What this implies is not a perfect organization producing a perfect service, but one that has a clear picture of what it is trying to do, a clear pattern of implementation and review, and constructive working relationships both inside and outside the organization legitimating and supporting the services provided.

If this is the ideal organization, there will be different ways of getting there. The 'new public management' (Pollitt 1993) required by modern organizations facing the demands of the 1990s and beyond may help. There is, naturally, no neat package that enables such an organization to emerge. But it seems likely that, as far as quality management is concerned, there will be two distinct streams of activity:

1 The development of a suitable infrastructure of culture, systems and decision-making structures and procedures.
2 Specific activities designed to maintain and improve the quality of the organization and its services.

Reform of the organizational infrastructure may, in some quality systems, particularly total quality management, be an integral part of the quality programme itself. However, to place reliance for improving the whole organizational infrastructure solely on such a programme is a risky strategy if, as is often the case, major change is needed. The quality policy then has to carry with it all other strategic policies.

Activities that might form part of a general organizational development programme will be needed but it might be better to develop them separately from specific quality-related activities. Then those activities – identification of interests and stakeholders, standard setting, service design, quality monitoring for example – could build on and be integrated with the general programme of development without making them interdependent – if one falls, everything falls.

An example of taking things one at a time can be found in Bradford City Council. In 1991, a successful quality pilot project began to improve the processing of housing benefits to private tenants. It built explicitly on the strengths of an earlier management development programme. This programme had been designed to improve communication and to build mutual trust between management and front-line. Without this earlier work, which enabled counter staff to feel confident that management would support the risk-taking involved in their quality pilot, it would almost certainly not have got off the ground.

Mapping quality systems

Putting aside for the moment the question of a broad organizational and management development programme of the type designed to build the infrastructure mentioned earlier, there are some important choices to be made when considering quality itself. With 'quality' high on the public agenda (Waldegrave 1993) and quality assessors (for BS 5750) thick on the ground (Freeman-Bell and Grover 1994), it is particularly important for public service managers to be able to assess a range of options and to choose one most suited to the particular needs and circumstances of their own organization. The contract culture is stampeding large and small contractors, public, private and voluntary, into trying to acquire certification that may be not only far too expensive compared with the potential benefits, but not even particularly relevant or useful. The situation is further confused by the fact that very different programmes may be encompassed within the same catch-all headings of quality control, quality assurance, total quality management and charters of one kind or another (Centre for Health Economics 1991a; Joss *et al.* 1992).

It is therefore important to look behind the names, at the content, coverage and declared purpose of the many different systems being marketed. A quality system ideally includes processes of:

- Identifying and involving key interests, stakeholders and actors.
- Developing and making explicit organizational values and objectives.
- Developing ideal (long-term) and attainable (medium-term) service standards.
- Organizational diagnosis: the service chain, service gaps, strengths and weaknesses.
- Identifying and choosing options for action.
- Implementation programme.
- Monitoring, evaluation and review.

How far do different quality systems encompass all these activities, especially the first; and what are the consequences if, as many of them are, they are only partial?

The Audit Commission's map

The Audit Commission (1993c) suggests that a comprehensive quality map consists of four main elements: (1) quality of communication; (2) specification; (3) delivery; and (4) 'people and systems'. Local authorities can use the map to plot what areas are or are not covered by their own quality systems. The implication is that all four areas should be covered if a satisfactory and workable quality programme is going to be able to take off.

Each dimension is itself broken down into several elements. The details of the Commission's approach can be criticized. For example, users are treated as if they had equal power with providers; excluded users are not considered; the significance of organizational cultures, styles and quality of internal communication is underplayed when considering the service chain, which appears to assume that the formulation of standards at each stage will be enough to make it effective.

However, the idea that quality concerns the wider community, and that clear service objectives are needed, as well as processes of consultation, organizational learning and high quality inputs (people and resources) are all useful reminders that not all organs of central government are exclusively concerned with charters, complaints and league tables.

Equally, the need to widen the vision of quality systems beyond those which concentrate almost exclusively on processes is usefully clarified. Customer care programmes, for example, tend only to cover the relationship with current users, leaving aside questions of service specifications and the quality of people and systems. Similarly, performance measurement systems, the document points out, are likely to focus on measurable targets linked to service processes or outputs, but generally omit relationships with consumers or the development of staff (inputs). Finally, the mapping process shows that quality assurance systems may cover processes and inputs, but generally exclude relationships with consumers and the key question of what the service is meant to do.

Methods and purposes of quality systems

The Centre for Health Economics, reviewing nearly 1500 'quality activities' reported by health districts (1991a: 32–35), also came up with four broad categories of quality systems. The Centre's categories, based on questionnaire and interview research in 1989, were different from those of the Audit Commission. It tried to divide quality activities according to the relationships between their defined aims and the way that quality was being defined, explicitly or by implication (noting that some activities would have more than one aim).

Thus health organizations whose definition of quality was mainly couched in terms of 'customer satisfaction' had focused their efforts on improving relations with users, on market research and, to some extent, on patient education. This education seems to have been generally producer-dominated, being more concerned with getting patients to understand (and accept?) what was being done medically than to clarify their expectations or to encourage questions or challenges to the service on offer – very much a medical model!

The other three categories of quality definition linked with quality improvement programmes arose from Donabedian's three dimensions of quality. Donabedian's own analysis underlined the interdependence of these three dimensions but, as the authors of the Centre for Health Economics' report say, the search for a respectable theoretical framework may not quite match with reality:

> The connection between the small-scale, practical efforts to improve quality at local level – in the ward, in the clinic, for example – and the overarching concepts of quality as expounded by writers on the subject are sometimes hard to see. Nevertheless, in providing an explanatory framework for the variety of efforts taking place, the broad concepts may provide essential motivation and guidance for those engaged in the practical tasks.
>
> (Centre for Health Economics 1991a: 35)

So these 'small-scale activities' could be divided between those covering the quality of the physical environment, those focusing on the quality of interpersonal relations and those aiming to improve overall service performance or technical/scientific quality. Under the first heading would come improvements to facilities; under the second, issues of staff training and participation and improving internal communications; under the third, the full gamut of procedures and guidelines, setting, reviewing and monitoring standards, improving 'efficiency' and carrying out pilot and test projects.

Inputs, throughputs, outputs and outcomes

Quality systems need to take into account the management model of inputs, throughputs (processes), outputs and outcomes. This model is widely used and is a further aid in distinguishing the focus of different quality programmes, both as an internal management process and as part of the client–contractor relationship.

For example, in organizations with a 'tight–loose' culture, politicians and strategic managers decide and monitor policy while operational managers make their own decisions about how to produce the service in order to achieve the desired results. The division of responsibilities for different parts of a quality programme can match this. The 'tight' centre might focus on outcomes, becoming involved in developing service standards and monitoring them; the 'loose' day-to-day managers would concentrate on throughputs and outputs, getting down to the detail of how to achieve the standards – the people, processes and procedures.

As far as contractual relationships are concerned, the Economic and Social Research Council's research programme on contracts (in progress at the time of writing) should throw light on whether purchasers in practice are in fact taking a belt and braces approach to contracts – specifying *both* that providers should have a certificated quality assurance system *and* setting out in fine detail the precise processes they should follow; or whether, on a more optimistic scenario (Walsh 1991), enough experience and trust develops between client and contractor for the contract specification to concentrate on broad outputs and outcomes, leaving the detailed responsibility for the quality of inputs (insofar as they are controllable), processes and immediate outputs to the contractor.

Charting quality initiatives

Quality initiatives – that is, activities designed to improve services in some way, whether explicitly defined under the heading of 'quality' or not – come in many shapes and forms, sometimes within an encompassing strategy, sometimes as the result of individual or departmental enthusiasms and values. Having toyed with the idea of producing a neat-looking table against which such initiatives could be charted, there are probably too many variables to be able to do this in a meaningful or helpful way. Instead, I propose a checklist. It is as follows:

> 1 *Is the quality system underpinned by values consistent with those on which the definition of quality is based?*

A public service organization may claim to be pursuing values of equality or empowerment. These can be undermined by, for example, failure to consult staff on crucial issues, or by 'participation' systems which favour the most articulate. It is not uncommon to find a local authority placing requirements on contractors or grant-aided voluntary organizations that it would be quite unable to fulfil itself. Many quality initiatives and 'customer care' programmes have fallen by the wayside or been implemented in the face of tremendous staff cynicism because of the contradiction that staff are being asked to value 'customers' while themselves being ignored. A quality implementation programme loses credibility if values are inconsistent.

> 2 *Are the objectives of the quality programme clear? What are the intended improvements, and are these (reasonably) consistent with other organizational objectives?*

Quality programmes seem very often to have been introduced for reasons that do not arise naturally from existing objectives. Indeed, their raison d'être may be extremely obscure, deriving from the latest management fashion, from the performance requirements of top managers, from external forces such as the apparent demands of the Government's Citizen's Charter policy. If this is the case, the programme is likely to be perceived to be a tokenistic, add-on set of activities with a narrow range of potential beneficiaries, among whom may or may not number the public.

> 3 *Does the quality programme arise from an organizational diagnosis?*

This question arises both in connection with the issues of appropriateness and practicability mentioned earlier – does the programme build on strengths and address weaknesses that actually exist? – and with the desire, among both managers and politicians, for instant solutions. The first can lead to dissonance. Customer care programmes may fail to acknowledge either the constraints with which most front-line staff have to struggle, or the very great skill and commitment that many staff already bring to their work as a matter of course. Systems imported wholesale from outside may not take account of specific circumstances: total quality management in the London Ambulance Service was abandoned because it was introduced as a top-down system with no consultation with staff or unions. Not surprisingly, staff resistance was enormous, especially as the timing of the programme coincided with major staff cuts (Ashrif 1993).

4 What sort of timescales are involved?
Short-termism can lead to early judgments and early disappointment. Programmes may be deemed not to have worked far too soon, because the time-consuming processes of change and internalization have not been allowed for or anticipated by the missionaries and top managers. Clarity about planned timescales helps to reduce uncertainty and to understand what is achievable at different stages.

5 Which key interests have been or should be involved at each stage of implementation?
A system that has the intention of changing staff behaviour but does not involve such staff in developing the system probably stands as little chance of success as a programme that depends on clarity of service objectives but does not involve the policy-makers. Quality improvement programmes by definition imply the need for change: it is the staff who must take responsibility for such change, so their involvement is essential.

As far as other interests are concerned, their identification should not be a mere intellectual exercise or – even more important – a tokenistic one. When the 'right' group has been brought together, it needs time for it to develop as a group. The draft guidance for 'quality action groups' (Norah Fry Research Centre 1990) suggests that considerable attention needs to be paid to building up the group cohesion, through familiarization and agenda-setting exercises. A roomful of strangers, with different levels of power, different expectations and experience, and different values, needs support to develop as a group. Mutual trust and understanding need to emerge before real progress on standard-setting, service-monitoring or policy advice (or whatever other activity is on the agenda) can be made.

6 Where is leadership and support coming from?
This is partly a question about the origins of the project. External consultants, for example, may be very enthusiastic about 'their' system – and able to communicate that enthusiasm to those they are working with during their time with the organization. When they leave, the project may collapse for lack of internal leadership and because other agendas encroach (Morgan and Everitt 1990). Conversely, pronouncements from senior officers can be crucial in giving staff the confidence to try out new techniques, to feel able to

'make mistakes' and to be clear about the overall purpose of what they are trying to do.

For example, traffic engineers in Hertfordshire tried out a new programme of consultation with parish councils and local communities. Although asking the public about their views appeared contrary to their professional training, first a new Director, then a new Chief Executive made it clear that this was the culture they were trying to instil throughout the organization. Individual traffic engineers felt they had backing for slightly unorthodox approaches.

7 What aspect of service is the quality programme intended to improve?

This is the question that the Audit Commission and the Centre for Health Economics were both examining. The Audit Commission was, in effect, making the policy/implementation cycle the basis of the analysis, while the Centre for Health Economics focused more on what definition of quality was being used. If implementation programmes are to avoid being accidentally partial, both aspects need to be covered. It is perfectly possible that action initially presented as some sort of panacea – the introduction of BS 5750 for example – is later seen as merely a starting point. Particular programmes will suit the needs of an organization at a particular time, but their limitations, intended coverage and links with longer term strategies need to be considered too.

8 Are measuring, monitoring and evaluation systems consistent with the rest of the programme?

This question will be examined in more detail in Chapter 7. However, with the current emphasis on (often externally imposed) quantitative performance indicators, considerable risks of distortion arise. In residential community care, for example, registration, measurement and audit systems may be the first thing to be put in place, while ideas about what sort of care consumers really need or want are left in abeyance. Pressure to meet quantitative targets, such as cutting down rent arrears or filling empty properties may put staff under contradictory pressures if, under a quality programme, they are also being expected to offer choice, to be sensitive to individual circumstances and to prevent homelessness.

The next step

If managers are to have tools at their disposal to help them improve the quality of their services, one of those tools is the ability to take a critical (not negative) stance and to be able to ask searching questions before becoming embroiled in day-to-day action.

A list such as that included here is not neutral: it arises from a particular perception of what quality in public services ought to be about. My perspective is that quality is an organizational, policy and cultural issue, not a managerial system to be brought in as the magic answer to a whole range of quite different – and difficult – problems.

Statements of intention may be 'big bang' in tone and universality. Successful implementation is likely to be slower and more gradual. It needs to be within a policy framework and it needs an underlying infrastructure to enable different implementation schemes to be introduced systematically. Is this total quality management? Inevitably, the answer is that it depends what you mean by total quality management! The next chapter looks at the meanings and practices in the current language of quality.

5

The practice of implementation

Some quality programmes

This chapter describes the main forms of quality programme, as they have emerged so far. It is natural for managers to want clear, preferably uncontroversial definitions of the different approaches, so that programmes suited to the needs of the organization can be chosen and implemented. It is not, of course, either possible or, I would suggest, desirable to find such definitions. Not possible, because what is done under the name of quality assurance or total quality management seems, from the little information available about actual practice, to differ quite considerably in reality. Not desirable, because the transferability of programmes developed to meet one purpose (profit maximization or market share) is unlikely to be entirely appropriate for another purpose (meeting needs, asserting the 'public interest' or providing 'public goods').

However, the general principles underlying different approaches are certainly of interest, and can lead to a better understanding of where to look for relevant experience from which to learn and develop programmes tailored to the particular needs of individual organisations. The Scylla of simplistic solutions and the Charybdis of reinvented wheels both need to be avoided if possible (this may not be a very good metaphor – I find on looking it up that Odysseus lost six of his sailors when trying to avoid both perils!).

Following the issues and questions raised in Chapter 4, the main programmes I shall examine are:

- Quality control.
- Quality assurance.

- Total quality management.
- Customer care.

I shall then look at some problem-solving and other techniques, before ending the chapter with a consideration of the structures and cultures that are – or may be – essential for the successful implementation of whichever programme is chosen.

Quality control (QC)

Quality control is perhaps the most familiar method of implementing quality. Its defining characteristic is that it focuses on the quality of a product or service *after* it has been produced. Based on a detailed specification, and complemented by product design and production processes intended to achieve that specification, what is actually produced is compared through an inspection process with what was intended to be produced (Caplen 1982). Consistency can be tested through sampling techniques, and conformance to specification can be tested through observation, physical tests and *post-hoc* consumer surveys.

An underlying assumption is that mistakes or variations will occur, and that product quality will only be achieved up to a certain percentage, with a certain number of faulty products slipping through. The control process – which may also include a complaints procedure – can be used to put things right, through rejection of the product or by reworking it. The psychology is one of 'putting things right' after the event.

It is not therefore a preventive strategy, though possibly rewards for good work or the fear of failure (especially if there are penalties attached, for example in a building contract) might provide pressure to 'get it right first time'. It is a process that can be applied at any stage in the quality chain, possibly to the detriment of mutual co-operation and understanding, but possibly to the benefit of the overall product if it thereby helps to identify weak links.

The obvious weakness of this approach is, first, that it is extremely difficult to apply to many services: once provided, services cannot usually be undone: the only remedy may be compensation (and possibly some organizational learning) or an enquiry. The pain of a poor quality service is displaced onto the recipient, who may have neither the power or the knowledge to challenge what has been done, nor, very often, the practical means of rectifying the fault. The wrong operation, a decision to take a child into care, an unsuitable housing allocation, may all be 'mistakes'. However, even if they can be clearly identified and perhaps rectified, they are capable of causing irreparable damage. A quality control system does not address this problem.

Second, as well as the practical issue that, for many services, especially the most personal ones, it is very difficult to 'inspect quality out', the long-term costs of quality control may be high. After all, each action is being taken twice, first with the initial process of production, then through the process of rectification. In addition there is the cost of inspection itself. 'Building quality in', as quality assurance is sometimes described, may be more realistic and, in the longer run, cheaper and more effective. The initial costs are likely to be higher, but the reduction in faults, together with the increased credibility and confidence between staff and consumers, would bring considerable benefits, financial and non-financial.

Third, the specification drawn up as the basis for the control process does not necessarily take account of the needs and wishes of consumers or of other stakeholders/interests. The overall approach tends to be statistical and, as Hutchins (1990: 106) notes in his comparison of the Western and Japanese approaches to quality control, quality control as understood in the West makes no reference to the role of people, as buyers or, indeed, as producers. (Hutchins notes that the Japanese Industrial Standard for quality control, JIS Z8101, specifically requires the product to meet buyers' demands and to involve the participation by all members of the workforce: it is a people-oriented system, compared with a systems and procedures orientation in the West.)

Despite these limitations, for those used to low quality public services, the existence of quality control techniques may provide much needed reassurance. Many services have traditionally been delivered on a take it or leave it basis, and the knowledge that some kind of inspection process is taking place, especially for products and services where human error is both possible and could have very serious consequences, symbolizes a new attitude and may even produce practical benefits for service users.

This is particularly important in situations where trust has not been developed between the provider and the recipient of services. It makes a lot of sense to have regular checks such as post-inspection for housing repairs, follow up of street rubbish collections, discussions of domiciliary services such as home care or meals on wheels with residents, or surveys of users of public spaces or swimming pools, to obtain feedback on whether specifications – standards – are being met.

For some services, especially where there are detailed technical specifications, some kind of expert and preferably independent inspection, such as the Community Inspectors who monitor environmental contracts in Harlow, is likely to be needed (Gaster 1995). In other cases, where the quality of the service may be easily judged by the layperson, 'market research' or more active feedback may be appropriate.

In some sense, all monitoring and measurement are a form of quality control and, as such, will be discussed in more detail in Chapter 7. However, it is worth noting here that such activities, when they involve consumers, assume that those being asked are willing to be frank in their replies. But it is no good asking patients what they think of their district nurse or their health visitor if the person asking the questions is known to be a close colleague of the worker about whom the questions are being asked. That way, a postinspection is likely to find 100 per cent satisfaction, as indeed happened in the case of a community health service unit in the mid-1980s. Similarly, the level of expectation needs to be defined in order to interpret the findings about satisfaction in any such survey.

Quality assurance (QA)

Taking a narrow view that service quality specifications can be precise enough for inspection – using statistical techniques and qualitative methods – there is a case for saying that, as long as the limitations are recognized, quality control does have a place within a quality implementation system. However, it would be much better for all concerned to get it right in the first place. This is what quality assurance is meant to be about.

Quality assurance is 'broadly the prevention of quality problems through planned and systematic activities (including documentation)' (Oakland 1989: 10). The Association of Metropolitan Authorities, urging the use of the British Standard 5750 Part Two by direct service organizations competing in compulsory competitive tendering contracts, suggested that the quality manual is actually 'the heart of the system' (Association of Metropolitan Authorities 1991a: 15). Monitoring or auditing the effectiveness of such quality assurance systems would be through 'discrepancy reports' – which sound remarkably like quality control procedures – and the emphasis, as with quality control, appears to be on the need for conformance and lack of variation.

Certificated systems of quality assurance are expensive to introduce and maintain. In the UK, the main certification process is the British Standard 5750. This was initially designed primarily to apply to manufacturing and has several parts. Part One covers design, production, installation and servicing, containing nineteen separate elements (Ellis 1988). It tends to be used by civil engineers and buildings and highways design departments for activities such as vehicle safety fencing, street lighting or the erection of street signs, having been 'encouraged' by the Department of Transport's policy of buying services from certificated contractors (Freeman-Bell and Grover, forthcoming). BS 5750 Part Two, which covers production and installation, is the system most commonly employed by local authorities, starting in Trading Standards departments in the early 1980s or even earlier and spreading to others, especially direct service organizations, in the late 1980s and early 1990s. Its application to social services is possible, as demonstrated by the certification of at least one social services residential home (Cassam and Gupta 1992). More recently (1991) a newer part (Part Eight), the equivalent of the International Standard ISO 9004–2, has been introduced. This is designed specifically for services, but does not yet seem to be widely used. It is very detailed, containing about 54 different elements under headings such as service characteristics, quality policy and objectives, personnel and other resources, systems and structures, documentation, customer relations and marketing processes, service design and delivery, control and consumer feedback, data collection and 'corrective action for nonconforming services'.

Freeman-Bell and Grover (1993a) found that 21 per cent of local authorities covered by their own 1992 survey had introduced BS 5750 in at least one department – usually trading standards or highways departments or in direct service organizations. However, they estimated that the costs were high. They report a 1992 survey by SGS Yardley, which found the direct financial costs (consultancy fees, paperwork, documentation, certification process etc) of companies with 75 employees to be, on average, £37,000. Further costs would be incurred for the inspection and recertification processes in subsequent years, but these might be offset by increased profits and reduced waste (Freeman–Bell and Grover 1993b). If BS 5750 were to be introduced comprehensively, it is easy to see how such costs would multiply in the large complex organizations, which many public services still are.

The cost and benefit considerations of quality assurance systems are complicated to calculate in the public sector, where they are often intangible, are certainly not measurable in terms of financial profit and where the longer-term benefits are probably more difficult to quantify than the immediate costs in terms of staff time, training and direct consultancy and certification fees.

If, however, the inherently beneficial characteristics of quality assurance could be proved, then the up-front costs would undoubtedly be worth it. What is disconcerting is that the benefits of the quality assurance approach as embodied in the BS 5750 Part Two have not yet been established. One reason for this is that it appears to emphasize systems and procedures at the expense of outputs and outcomes. Hutchins (1990: 39) quotes a gas appliance company whose systems were classed as 'faultless', yet 60 per cent of the product had to be reworked before it could leave the factory. With neither consumers nor staff automatically involved in the specification and design process, the question must be asked: 'assurance of what?'

Ellis (1988: 6) takes a simple definition of quality assurance from the manufacturing industry as being the process of ensuring that the product consistently achieves customer satisfaction. He warns, possibly in vain, against overcomplicating the concept. He sees quality assurance as the antithesis of quality control, enabling service producers themselves to exercise internal control, as opposed to being inspected externally. Yet he also points out the difficulties of knowing who has to be satisfied, especially as access to services in the 'caring professions' tends to be controlled by 'we know best' professionals: however altruistic in intent, they tend towards secrecy and complacency when thinking about developing and auditing the quality of their own services (see also Pollitt 1988).

Despite the self-evidently good intention of 'building quality in', some disadvantages of a quality assurance approach can be identified, especially if the system used is a standard one rather than one built up from inside. These include:

- The overemphasis on written procedures and controls. While some procedures are necessary to ensure consistency and fairness, the detailed documentation required can in practice be heavily bureaucratic and time-consuming: it could even inhibit innovation and experiment and reinvent the old 'watch your back' cultures of the past.
- The failure to consider what the service is for: what is the 'product' that the excellent procedures are intended to underpin? In terms of the Audit

Commission's map, quality assurance only covers two areas: the quality of delivery and the quality of people and systems. Quality assurance is therefore limited in how far it can cover all the quality issues likely to be faced by a public service organization.

- Quality assurance systems tend in practice to be top-down or externally imposed. The workforce, consumers and residents are not actually included. This means that it may be difficult to convince the workforce of their relevance or utility, depending on the relationship between management and staff and on the public reasons for introducing the system.
- The high setting-up costs, in both financial terms and in staff time. If, as is increasingly the case in the contract culture, BS 5750 certification becomes a near requirement for service producers, smaller organizations, especially those in the voluntary sector, could be driven out of the market altogether: the costs, in relation to the need for day-to-day financial viability over very short timescales, are too high.

Much of the criticism of quality assurance systems is focused on certificated methods, especially the British Standard. However, while recognizing the limitations of this approach, quality assurance does force organizations to think about the details of their products and services in a way that they had never done before. This experience was confirmed by the direct service organizations (Association of Metropolitan Authorities 1991a), who had already experienced similar effects from the first round of compulsory competitive tendering. It was very hard work at the time, but the long-term change in staff attitudes and the overall organizational culture was thought to be very positive. In these cases, the quality assurance process was seen as a vehicle for change and clarity of purpose, just as the tortuous process of developing service level agreements has helped central service providers (finance departments, committee administration and a huge range of other support services identified by CIPFA) to understand where they come in the quality chain, and to change their relationships with internal 'consumer' departments (Association of Metropolitan Authorities 1991b).

Quality assurance does not have to be carried out through a set system such as the British Standard. It can be developed internally, to suit the needs and situation of each organization. Quality assurance can be a mechanistic and possibly manipulative process aiming to win contracts, and not necessarily to provide a better service. However, if it is seen as developmental and preventative, it can be very positive, incorporating the idea of analysing the service process, of identifying procedures that will ensure consistency within whatever value system has been espoused, and providing staff with appropriate training and tools for self-evaluation. These are all part of the 'good practice' that few would dispute is needed in the modern management of public services.

Is it really necessary to go any further? Will quality assurance suffice, or should the aim be for a more holistic system that, rather than changing the culture as a by-product of the new procedures, has the explicit aim of creating a new culture within which service quality will flourish and improve? This is the somewhat missionary approach of the advocates of total quality management – TQM for short.

Total Quality Management (TQM)

Within the private sector, total quality management is, as its name implies, a management system. Its main feature, in intention at least (as we shall see, there are several different approaches), is that it is a comprehensive system, even, its proponents claim, a philosophy. Quality has to be everyone's business. According to its advocates, some of the key features are that there should be obsessional commitment (Oakland 1989: 16) from the top, understanding from the bottom, that there should be well developed systems and training, supportive management, and that policy objectives should be clear. The ultimate aim is to achieve zero defects: failures will not be accepted.

Paradoxically, some inconsistencies arise from the desire for consistency. A key element of the kind of total quality management system proposed by Oakland is the statistical process control beloved of Deming: mistakes are not tolerated and the reduction of variance – through training, reducing the number of suppliers, the careful design of systems and making people responsible only for those processes they can control – is the ultimate objective:

> SPC [statistical process control] is not only a tool kit. It is a strategy for reducing variability, the cause of most quality problems: variation in products, in times of deliveries, in ways of doing things, in materials, in people's attitudes, in equipment and its use, in maintenance practices, in everything. Control by itself is not sufficient. Total quality management requires that the process should be improved continually by reducing its variability.
>
> (Oakland 1989: 180)

This implies a non–risk-taking culture: risks mean mistakes. Yet at the same time two other requirements, which form the basis of the continuous improvement (one of the key characteristics of total quality management), are the need for innovation and development. For the private sector and all those now competing to be service providers, innovation is essential to give a competitive edge. A developmental approach is also essential for public utilities and services needing to ensure their continued ability to respond to public requirements and statutory demands. The pressure to standardize and the pressure to innovate could well conflict, causing tension at both personal and organizational levels.

It may be helpful at this point to set out some of the main features of total quality management systems, as gleaned from a variety of writers and practitioners:

- *Basic features*: a total quality approach is expected to embrace not only quality systems but also the actual processes of production, the style and method of management and the active participation of the workforce. Although not necessarily spelt out in this way, the organizational culture needs to be participative, not hierarchical and authoritarian (see, for example, Hutchins, Chapter 3).

- *Stages*: there several stages in total quality management. These are variously described as: awareness; assessment or diagnosis; planning and preparation; implementation, including education and training and the development of commitment and understanding within the organization; a stage of continuous or intensive improvement (over a period of two to three years) and a final stage of review, leading to a renewal of the process of continuous improvement.
- *Staff roles*: leadership and commitment at the top; teamwork and training among the staff – a Japanese culture; innovation and quality groups and possibly special staff responsibilities (internal consultant role?) – but Deming warns against hiving off responsibility where it can be isolated and ignored by other staff.
- *Methods*: focus on variations and mistakes that can be controlled (and are not necessarily caused by human error). Focus on chronic (i.e. continuing and consistently damaging) problems rather than firefighting. Use of problem-solving processes and techniques, staff ideas and suggestions, quality teams, management of change and the development of new organizational cultures.
- *Aim*: to 'delight the customer'.

Types of total quality management

Within these broad characteristics, differences appear. Susan Whittle (1992), for example, studying the manufacturing sector, identified four variants with very different implications for the organizations involved and for the managers responsible for implementing the systems. These types are planning, learning, visionary and transformation total quality management: behind them lie different origins and champions, different methods and different aims. Not surprisingly, Whittle found that they also emerged with different strengths and weaknesses, which could affect their long term resilience and effectiveness. While there are some parallels with the scientific, managerial and consumerist approaches to quality identified by Pfeffer and Coote (1991), there was no hint among the manufacturing companies studied by Whittle of any democratic approach – Pfeffer and Coote's fourth category and the one that underlies this book.

Whittle's first category – the *planning* approach to total quality management – focuses on variance control. She found that it was often initiated (owned) by engineers and technical staff or by quality managers. Their aim is to reduce waste and increase productivity. They tend to be more operational than strategic. Although Whittle felt that the transferability of scientific total quality management to the public sector would be limited, there are some areas of activity where, like quality control, its application might not be seen by consumers as a bad thing. Getting routine activities right, within a framework of knowing what is required and possible – hospital appointments systems come to mind – would be a cause of considerable rejoicing among those who suffer interminable waits, uncertainty or simply failure to communicate by those with the power to make decisions.

Second, Whittle identified *learning* total quality management systems. These arose from an organizational developmental perspective and were championed by human resource (personnel) managers. The emphasis here is on the staff, encouraging their participation and developing performance appraisal systems and better working environments. Again, this approach is seen as more operational than strategic, being focused on individuals. However, here, rather than emphasizing the elimination of mistakes, the aim is to create a learning environment. If this enables the organization to become flexible and responsive enough to be able to tackle a range of strategic – and changing – objectives, it has considerable attractions for public service organizations.

It is certainly a useful and practical starting point, and it is this method that Bradford City Council began with in 1991. Their programme was not actually called total quality management. Using a systematic pilot project approach, its great advantage was its practicability, being holistic in sentiment but not requiring the whole organization to take everything on at once. The idea was that groups of staff in each main department would identify a problem area where a quality programme of analysis and action, supported by senior management, would be initiated. Others in the department (and the council as whole) would learn and build from these. While requiring support and understanding from the top, it was a programme that consciously avoided having to depend on passing training and information down from top to bottom. Impetus and direction would have been dissipated by such an approach, the Bradford officers thought.

The top-down approach is Whittle's third category of TQM, the *visionary*. It tends to be owned by senior management. The idea of 'mission' features strongly here, and communication and training is in the cascade (or Chinese whispers?) mode, being passed down but not, it seems, up the line. This will sound familiar to any organization that has suffered a series of management initiatives that have failed to get staff involved or committed – like numerous customer care initiatives, management by objectives, or the overdogmatic equal opportunities policies of the 1980s, which, with changes of leadership and the pressures of the market, are being quietly sidelined in the 1990s (Solomos and Back 1993).

Fourth, and finally, Whittle identified a *transformation* model of total quality management. It was not clear who in an organization 'owned' this model, but its intention, insofar as it could be defined, seemed to be to create an organization that could take on any or all of the three previously described approaches. This, over a long period – ten or twelve years or even longer – would enable it to predict and respond to change, take on new ideas, and create a new mind-set among managers and staff. Its weakness was that it could appear to be unfocused and possibly too challenging.

This kind of total quality management, while comprehensive and flexible, hardly qualifies for the description of total quality management. Any organization taking such an approach to management, staff development and production of services is surely in the process of some kind of comprehensive management and organizational development programme. This is a necessary part of the infrastructure for any organization wishing to think seriously about improving service quality, a foundation for the details of explicit quality programmes to be laid. However, it is important not to become so wide-ranging that any activity directed towards general improvement is labelled a 'quality' activity, as Donabedian observed in relation to definitions of quality. It then becomes too hard to focus on exactly what could and should be done specifically in the name of quality.

No simple definitions

As Joss et al. (1991, 1992) found in their evaluations of eight Department of Health 'demonstration site' grant-funded total quality management initiatives, the interpretations of the total quality management language varied widely from site (that is, hospital) to site. This is not surprising, arising as it does from the fact that there is no single definition of total quality management. Yet several gurus (Deming, Crosby, Juran, Oakland) lay claim to the notion as if it were an objective certainty.

The development of holistic, integrated systems for improving service quality does seem desirable. My preference is to see the different features of quality identified in Figure 1.1 as issues that any organization serious about quality would be grappling with. Calling them total quality management smacks of sloganizing and mystification. It seems to me to be totally unnecessary and likely to make key people feel excluded, in an area of policy and management where exactly the opposite is needed. For staff and the public to be told that they do not 'understand' total quality management is unnecessarily alienating, yet this seems to be the approach adopted by missionaries, trainers and consultants. It is enough to put anyone off.

Customer care

Customer care programmes can, like other quality programmes, be interpreted and implemented very differently. There is relatively little information about their origins and implementation, although written 'customer care' statements can be picked up in a wide range of circumstances, from reception areas in social services and housing departments to your local post office or bank. They seem mainly to concentrate on the immediate impression that a service provider makes on the 'customer'. In this sense they could be a contribution to improving the interpersonal or non-technical dimension of quality. This is a dimension that has tended to be neglected in the definitions of quality deriving from the manufacturing industry where, as we have seen, the more scientific and technical aspects have been the main focus. So it could be argued that customer care programmes provide a useful counterbalance to an approach that might otherwise overemphasize the role of the professionals and bureaucrats, to the detriment of those receiving or potentially receiving the services in question.

Unfortunately, many customer care programmes appear (but this is anecdotal evidence) to have been introduced in a very top-down way as a substitute for thinking deeply about quality as a whole. Such programmes have tended to put the front-line staff under the spotlight, while the systems and back-up to enable those staff to provide a better service have not been attended to. In addition, the role of consumers, especially those not in direct receipt of service, or who may have an interest as a citizen rather than as a consumer, is treated as passive rather than active. Assumptions are made by senior managers as to the desired staff behaviours that might minimize trouble from the public, rather than creating a culture where public needs and demands are both listened and responded to.

Some programmes going under the heading of customer care, such as that being introduced in Hackney Council in 1992, or the Nottingham City Council approach where customer care forms part of a wider 'learning organization' strategy, are in fact quite comprehensive, including consultation with consumers, standard-setting procedures and action to remedy failure. However, the general picture of customer care programmes is that they have a much narrower aim of teaching staff how to be better gatekeepers and, if necessary, scapegoats for failings elsewhere in the organization. The wearing of badges and uniforms and the 'service with a smile' approach to customer care can be a particularly depressing example of a quality programme that could have been designed to increase staff cynicism, not to improve services. They could also have the effect, as the Chief Executive of South Somerset District Council noted, of emphasizing consumerism at the expense of democracy:

> The consumerist approach can degenerate badly into an imposed 'charm school' of smiles, badges and piped music, leaving fundamental questions of power and responsibility unanswered . . . Politics becomes an unnecessary hindrance if local government is seen simply as a convenient instrument for delivering a bundle of services.
>
> (Gaster and Taylor 1993: 25)

However, to look on the positive side, many of these programmes in the public sector have possibly signalled the beginning of a shift in attitude, which may provide the potential for a more thought through and comprehensive approach to quality improvements, particularly if some kind of review is built into the programme.

Returning to the Audit Commission's quality map, the idea of focusing on the direct relationship between service provider and 'customer' (a word that, despite its limitations, may at least symbolize a shift away from the dependent 'client' approach) touches on a very limited aspect of quality. If it is seen as part of a wider programme, where it is not only 'customers' who are valued and involved, but also front-line and other traditionally undervalued staff, then it has some hope of success. Otherwise, in the classic Lipsky analysis, it is almost certain to be one of those programmes that is implemented tokenistically, if at all, leaving top managers wondering where they have gone wrong, and lower level staff even less trusting of the intentions of those above them.

Tools for the job

It is perhaps in the arena of implementation that the choices available to managers become the most diffuse, the most difficult, yet the most prone to simplistic and partial solutions. The development of policy and practice to improve quality requires at the very least a systematic and strategic approach. Ideally, processes of implementation should arise directly from an analysis of where the organization now is, and what needs to be done to achieve explicit quality objectives, informed by explicit values. It would be very rare for ready-made solutions to be directly transferable from elsewhere, especially between service sectors where the ethical, political and practical situations are so different.

Each organization needs, then, to understand the range of different approaches that might be pursued. A particular differentiation might be made between those activities designed to catch people out – the legalistic contracts or service level agreements, the use of control and inspection, the emphasis on accreditation and league tables; and methods which, with a more integrated approach both to processes and to outputs/outcomes, aim to 'build quality in'. While it is argued (Stewart and Walsh 1989) that the quality assurance method is more appropriate to public services, and while proponents of both quality assurance and total quality management will (rightly) argue that, at least in the longer run, preventive action is cheaper than corrective action, it seems likely that in practice a mixture of approaches will be needed, in different departments or at different times.

In Chapter 4 I suggested a set of questions that might be applied to any quality system to help managers decide whether it is right for them. At this stage of the discussion, it is appropriate to try to pull together the common features that may be helpful to those same managers and to the politicians (where they exist) on whose policies the practices of quality must be based.

The suggestions that follow assume a certain model of quality. It sees the involvement of staff and the public as fundamental. It is based on an assumption that staff in public service organizations will have a commitment to altruistic values – the old-fashioned but not yet extinct public service ethos – and that, despite the descriptive/prescriptive analyses of the public choice theorists (see Dunleavy 1991), they are not simply employed to take rational decisions that will maximize the benefits of their actions to themselves. All this does, however, depend on organizational values, and it is likely that in the increasingly divided public services, the motivation of the purchasers of services will not necessarily be the same as those of the providers, particularly when the latter do not come from a public service tradition.

Nevertheless, there will be some common features in any implementation system. I suggest that these fall into three groups:

- Techniques.
- Structures.
- Cultures.

Quality techniques

Within any quality system, different techniques and processes may be used. They can serve three main purposes:

- Diagnosis of what is required.
- Maintaining quality.
- Application of 'best practice' – learning from others.

Problem-solving, diagnostic techniques

Oakland and other writers on total quality management stress the use of problem-solving techniques to assess the present state of play and identify which problems can most profitably and practically be tackled. A SWOT (strengths, weaknesses, opportunities, threats) analysis helps to identify the main problems, and to demonstrate that not everything has to be seen negatively. There *are* opportunities as well as threats. Pareto analysis helps to discover the 20 per cent of the problems which, if rectified, would produce the greatest long-term benefit for the organization. Bar charts and scatter diagrams show countable variations from the norm. Brainstorming helps the qualitative side of the diagnosis.

A popular problem-solving technique is that invented by Kaoru Ishikawa, the inventor of quality circles in the 1950s. It was in 1943 that he invented the fishbone diagram. This helped workers to analyse the causes of problems in terms of whether they were caused by 'men, methods, machines, materials'. Such an analysis would lead to the questions 'why, when, who, what and how?' in order to identify remedial action (Hutchins 1990: 270).

Once the priorities for action are clear, explicit goals and targets can be set and further techniques used to pinpoint the focus of future effort. Data can be collected systematically (though there is of course a danger of insisting too heavily on quantitative approaches, a point to be taken up in Chapter 7). Or a force field analysis can be constructed, helping to demonstrate the positive forces to be built upon (staff commitment, good relationships with consumers, support from councillors), as well as any negative forces to be countered (lack of training strategy, non-involvement of unions, remoteness of senior management, poor communication systems) in making progress from the present to the intended state.

These and other techniques would be particularly useful at an early, diagnostic stage in the quality process, though as the workbooks for the quality action groups developed by the Norah Fry Research Centre (1990) show, it may be necessary at any time to go back to the diagnostic and problem-solving activities, as a check on what is happening, or if something is not working out as planned.

Quality working groups

However, these actions cannot be undertaken in a vacuum, and this is where a second group of techniques, the use of quality groups, comes in. Groups can come in all shapes. As Joss *et al.* (1991, 1992) found, they may be mainly top-down, top management groups with appointed membership, or they may be bottom-up groups generally composed of volunteers. It is helpful to have a named person who feels a responsibility for keeping the policy on track, but the appointment of specialist quality managers can be problematic. Will they provide the necessary leadership and support for the organization or will their appointment enable other staff to breathe a sigh of relief and assume that quality is being 'done' by someone else? Unless there is very widespread support and commitment to the quality policy, the likelihood is that quality managers will be isolated and quality policies marginalized – another parallel with the equal opportunities experience of the 1980s.

In Bradford, the Director of Social Services took responsibility at the corporate level, ensuring that senior managers kept quality on the agenda, while a corporate policy officer played an enabling role in helping individual quality initiatives get going. In some local authorities, secondments are used, but in others, social service inspectors seem to be taking on the role, at least as regards community care. This possibly signalled to staff that quality was to be a process of control rather than development.

Even if the process concentrates on the use of groups, the problem of the group members becoming isolated from other staff is likely to arise, however the group is formed and maintained. Awareness of this possibility, and arrangements for feedback and accountability, particularly in mixed groups where a range of stakeholders is represented, can counteract the lack of ownership which might otherwise be felt by those who do not 'belong'.

The Norah Fry work underlined the need not only for the appointment of a group leader and the clear identification of key 'stakeholders' (including, most importantly, service users), but also for the group to have a chance to develop as a group, and for the leader to be familiar with and able to handle group processes.

Quality circles

Quality circles – Kaoru Ishikawa's second main contribution to quality development – are a special form of working group. According to David Hutchins, a major advocate of this technique for use in the British industry, they are not simply problem-solving groups, but a way of bringing back the notion of craftsmanship into the world of manufacturing. Like the other forms of quality implementation discussed earlier in this chapter, the name 'quality circle' tends to be used fairly loosely: indeed, with his missionary approach, Hutchins suggests that those circles that fail cannot have been true circles in the first place!

According to his definition (derived from Ishikawa among others) quality circles are formed voluntarily from employees doing the same sort of work – generally six to ten people – accountable in some way to all those in that work area. Led by a supervisor, they are expected to identify, analyse and present solutions to problems within their work, sometimes for management action, sometimes for action by the circle itself. They would be likely to go through the phases of problem identification and solution, monitoring, innovation – that is, introducing improvements to services, having concentrated on preventative activities earlier on – and, in the ideal type (which Hutchins doubts has been reached anywhere in the West), the quality circles are expected to reach a phase of self-control, trusted and supported by management to make their own decisions. This implies a regime of devolved management, to be discussed below.

Hutchins is adamant that quality circles should not be introduced until the policy and culture is right. Indeed, he suggests that 90 per cent of UK circles fail: a prime cause is seen as the failure to undertake full quality circle training, preferably using external, specialist consultants.

Barrie Dale, in his research on quality circles in the early 1980s (Dale, 1986) found the special role of quality circle leaders or facilitators to be crucial, though he also found that most organizations had problems in maintaining impetus at some stage.

Certainly quality circles are no simple solution, requiring a good deal of support (including the legitimation of time to attend) and assuming both an understanding with trades unions that their roles will not compete, and a reasonably steady workforce – both of which could be assumed in Japan where they started, but are not (except in times of recession) necessarily a factor in Western employment patterns. Even if they work in the way Hutchins advocates, it seems to me that quality circles are limited in the contribution they may make to an overall quality policy. They may provide a useful and important starting point to thinking more widely about very specific issues – or perhaps they could take on issues identified by others? – but they appear to reflect a rather self-contained approach to quality improvement. There is no hint of consumer involvement at any stage in the process, for example, and they can only work on problems entirely within their control. There is, as far as I can discover, no acknowledgment of the quality chain and thus the need for the co-operation and involvement of people and teams beyond the immediate work environment.

So, while improved quality will not happen by itself, and the setting up of working groups of various kinds is almost certainly an essential feature of any quality programme, there are clearly several pitfalls to be avoided. The cheerful announcement that quality circles are to be established would be unlikely to be enough to produce effective implementation.

Learning from others

A third set of techniques arises from the need not to keep reinventing wheels and to be able to learn constructively from others. The benchmarking approaches being promulgated through both the Audit Commission (through the quality exchange) and the Welsh Office (Bullivant and Naylor 1992) both suggest that, while one would not necessarily be trying to take over lock stock and barrel the approach developed by another organization, an analysis of processes required to produce a service (the quality chain) is likely to show that some areas of activity (the processing of routine requests for action, efficient reception activities, managing a residential home) could well have parallels in unlikely places. A detailed study of the practices of organizations well-known for their success in specific activities could produce ideas as to how one's own organization might change its approach. The only difficulty here, emphasized by the problem of commercial confidentiality that is currently clouding discussion between service providers, is whether organizations are willing to be open about how they do things. An element of mutual trust – and the choice of an organization that is unlikely to be in direct competition with one's own – might be a way round this problem.

Organizational structures

The structures within which public services have been delivered in the past have tended to be large, divided into departments and sections, bureaucratically and/or professionally hierarchical, and difficult for the outsider to penetrate, whether as consumer, resident or potential co-worker. Much of the debate about quality in the public services has been about systematically developing systems and processes – and structures – which, by breaking down or crossing traditional barriers, can make the service to the consumer more comprehensible, better integrated and more sensitive to the needs and desires of those who pay for the services – the public.

The nature and variety of values that may be propelling public service organizations in one direction or another were explored in Chapter 1. Although there are many areas of difference, it can be assumed that, contained within the widely shared objective of the efficient, fair allocation and use of resources, there is also a common need for accessible, integrated and responsive services. These, together with such other service attributes as reliability, are likely to be among most people's definitions of public service quality.

There are in addition strong forces pushing many public service authorities (purchasers *and* providers where that split has taken place) towards more open, consultative and sometimes participative relationships with the public. As far as central government is concerned, such consultation is seen mainly in terms of direct users and, perhaps, carers. Local authorities and some health authorities have been seeing their relationship with the public in much broader terms, frequently invoking the word 'citizen' to include all those with a legitimate interest in but perhaps not an immediate involvement with particular services. The discussion in Chapter 2 of the potential role in quality policy and practice of people and groups with interests in the service demonstrated the need for structures that would support involvement of the public. The nature of public services, especially those that are compulsory or rationed, increases the need to take active steps to counter alienation, especially of those groups that tend to be excluded from routine consultation processes.

A further point, quoted earlier from Parasuraman *et al.* (1985) in relation to the need to close the gaps in the quality chain, is the importance of maximizing the decision-making authority of those with responsibility to deliver a service or part of a service. How far are the gaps between policy and practice caused by hierarchical management and bureaucratic procedures? How far, in other words, can or should power be devolved down the structure, both within the management structure and, where applicable, within political structures too?

The discussion of the four main types of quality system – quality control, quality assurance, total quality management and customer care – underlined the importance of gaining involvement and ownership by staff. Those concerned with public services, such as Cassam and Gupta, are equally clear that no system will work unless there is some form (or forms) of participation by the public.

Devolution and decentralization

The implication of all these analyses is that devolved structures within clear and relevant policy frameworks – the tight–loose approach favoured by Peters and Waterman and most writers on decentralization – are probably the most appropriate for the development of an effective quality policy. There is, I think, a close relationship between quality, decentralization and devolution (Gaster 1991a, 1992a). However, decentralization is not a panacea, whatever form it takes (and many different models are possible) – it is a means to an end, not an end in itself. It may be one of several options available to meet different policy objectives (Gaster and Hoggett 1993). Devolved management is also possible within centralized structures. There is a strong case, based on the values and general policy objectives mentioned above, to develop organizational structures that are conducive to both staff ownership of policies and to staff commitment to implement them as originally intended – to 'drive out fear', as Deming would have said. This implies the need both for appropriate structures of control and responsibility and appropriate cultures too.

While there may well be a need for some localized structures to relate to the needs of different geographical communities and neighbourhoods, other ways of responding to communities of need and of interest will also be needed. Local offices – one-stop shops – can provide services that cover part of or the whole of a service chain, depending on the length of the chain and the facilities provided locally. What those in the local offices will need to be good at is bridging the gaps, making the links along the chain, with the 'back line' within their own organizations and with other organizations (for example, as contractual providers or co-operative collaborator).

It is debatable whether changing the structure will be enough on its own. Cassam and Gupta (1992) expressed concern that in the haste to set up purchaser and provider organizations within social services departments, a divisiveness that is exactly contrary to the needs of a quality assurance policy would be created. Certainly, there are signs of recentralization and respecialization after two decades of attempts to work more generically and more locally in social services.

The experience of decentralization in local government (see Burns *et al.* 1994) also demonstrates the need to give as much attention to processes of change and to developing a new culture − both at the centre and in the neighbourhoods − as to finding sites for offices, appointing all-purpose managers or setting up comprehensive but possibly unfriendly computer systems.

If an infrastructure for quality can be identified, the notion of small teams of people with clear areas of responsibility, accountability and control does appear to be a common feature of the pronouncements of all the quality gurus. The lines of consultation and accountability out to the public and, in local government, to elected representatives is not, of course, mentioned by those same gurus, but is one that would, for public services, need to be firmly in place. Consumer loyalty − not the same thing as involvement but important none the less − is an inherent part of service quality: it is where the whole idea started. Generating that loyalty is far easier at the local and the team level than it is in 'faceless bureaucracies'. The study of decentralization in Islington and Tower Hamlets by Paul Hoggett and Robin Hambleton (Burns *et al.* 1994) underlined the personal 'accountability through visibility' that emerges from proximity and accessibility of a neighbourhood office. They also found evidence of the ability to give a better service to people who know and trust those with the power of decision, because they were receiving better information on a more continuous basis, enabling the accumulation of evidence on which to base, for example, welfare benefits or housing benefits claims.

Organizational cultures

All public services are under immense pressure most of the time. At the same time as resources are reduced, demand increases, for demographic, economic and social reasons. It is tempting in these circumstances to revert to the old ways of working, where the (implied) objective was to get rid of people as quickly as possible, to treat them 'as a number' (Gaster 1993a), to shift the blame or responsibility if at all possible − and above all, to avoid meeting the public. However, such ways of working do not improve relationships with the consumer − nor with co-workers − and the likely result is that those who have no wish for public services to survive and prosper will be given every reason for reducing them still further. Survival, as was suggested in Chapter 1, is as good a reason as any for embracing a quality policy.

The culture of an organization is represented through the values and customs to which all employees are expected to conform, as much through techniques of socialization as through more explicit training and induction programmes. The use of power and influence to ensure conformity to the dominant group's way of thinking makes the role of formal and informal leaders highly significant.

Processes of organizational change, whether or not accompanied by structural change of the kind discussed above, almost by definition require changes in attitudes and behaviour. They also tend to generate high levels of resistance through processes of dynamic conservatism (Schon 1971), unless the culture is already one that is used to and even welcomes change. Few public service organizations are yet in this category, though much of the effort within strategic management is directed towards creating organizations of just this kind (Local Government Management Board 1993a). But all quality implementation policies are necessarily processes of organizational change.

The need for an appropriate culture is stressed by all writers on quality, whether they are writing about the public, private or voluntary sectors. Whatever quality system is being introduced, whatever definitions of quality are used, there are some common features. Their importance will vary from one organization to another, perhaps, but the need to get away from blaming management, from macho management, and from hierarchical management are all seen as key to the success and effectiveness of the pursuit of quality.

Nurturing networks, encouraging collaboration, working in teams, creating multidisciplinary groups and an enabling style of leadership tend to be the desired qualities and attributes of the management–employee relationships. Clear commitment, understanding and a sense of direction from the top are vital, otherwise groups can become isolated and disheartened. A culture of mutual trust, where communication is open, honest and explicit, is equally necessary.

This sounds almost too good to be true. What is encouraging is that some organizations – or, more accurately, parts of organizations – have been able to develop an atmosphere where employees feel valued and listened to, and where relationships with the public are beginning to reflect these internal changes. The idea of treating colleagues – or others in the quality chain – as customers can seem rather odd. But if the effect is to ensure that requests for information or action are treated with proper respect and practical responsiveness, then the internal atmosphere of fobbing off, which gets translated only too easily into front-line negative behaviour, can become the unacceptable culture, to be condemned as inappropriate and organizationally undermining. Good communication and the development of trust, especially in senior management, but also between departments, professionals and other in-built groupings, are essential.

This section seems to be becoming a tract on good behaviour. Its point is merely to reiterate and pull together the need for attitudes and behaviour, especially the latter, to match the ideals of a policy that aims to improve the service to the consumer and community. Chris Skelcher (1992: 113) suggests that:

Developing a service culture is about redefining the relationships between groups. In the process some will feel that they are losing power,
others that they are taking a risk by accepting the invitation to play a
more active role in the organisation.

Through processes of socialization, leadership and training, staff can feel
supported – given time and commitment – to make the changes needed. If
quality policies are to be implemented in a way that makes them durable,
renewable and appropriate, the right organizational culture must be the key.

Implementing quality: some final thoughts

In the last two chapters, I have tried to analyse approaches to implementation
in a way that will be helpful to managers of public services looking for ways
forward. I have suggested that there is a set of questions, or criteria, that might
be applied to see if any proposed system is relevant to a particular organization,
bearing in mind its current state, its underlying values and its intended objectives. At the same time, I have also tried to demystify some of the language
surrounding the apparently scientific systems advocated by many writers on
quality, noting how the same words are used in different ways, giving them a
range of meanings and implications for action.

I have a wariness about slogans. This leads me to believe that any organization wishing to develop and implement a quality policy should do so on its
own. They should pick eclectically from the experience of others but not
swallow ideas wholesale without reflecting on their suitability in what might be
very different circumstances.

In the next chapter, I shall be examining the issue of standards and the
things that go with them – charters, service promises or whatever language may
be used to express the exact nature of the service the public may be led to
expect. I shall be particularly concerned about the question of where the
standards are coming from, and the dangers of losing the flexibility, incentives
for innovation or the sensitivity to different circumstances that are surely the
hallmarks of a high quality public service. At this point, it is the partial nature of
many of the known approaches to implementation – quality control, quality
assurance and total quality management, to say nothing of customer care, that
concern me.

At the same time, working towards consistency and reliability does not
have to be the same as working towards conformity and standardization. So my
concern that standards may be developed at the expense of variety is also
reflected in my concern that some systems, especially if transferred too readily
from the private sector, will positively discourage risk-taking and non-
conformity at a time when, within the needs of an equitable service, such
approaches are in all too short supply.

6
Quality standards

Introduction

All service organizations and the people in them work to some kind of stand-ard. Sometimes these are derived from the values and objectives of the organ-ization, sometimes from the professional training undergone earlier in life, sometimes from personal values. Such standards may be high, low, variable, unpredictable and contradictory. Their main feature is that, unlike the specifi-cations for manufactured goods, they tend not to be explicit. If they are written down, it will often be in the form of a code of practice, for internal or external consumption, with different degrees of enforcement, public knowledge or consensus from those they affect.

The standards to be discussed in this chapter are not of this kind. They are the standards that take the form of a written statement available to both staff and the public. They can include basic principles about how the service will operate, together with specified targets as the basis for public complaint and redress and to provide criteria for measurable achievement.

Published standards do not necessarily express actual cultural values and aims. They may be the tip of the quality iceberg, reflecting a well developed organizational commitment to improvements across the board. They may, however, represent a cynical attempt to forestall criticism and to deflect atten-tion onto front-line staff and away from the policy-makers. Or, to abandon the conspiracy theory and concentrate on something nearer to reality, their con-struction may be a first step in making explicit to staff and the public what it is that the organization is setting out to achieve. In this case, publishing such standards may lead towards the development of appropriate management and policy systems to support their implementation. Finally, published standards may simply reflect the statutory minimum required by law, often already known to the professionals and the inspectors but not, except when being enforced through the courts, a conscious part of the public's knowledge of the service.

Standard-setting can form part of any quality implementation system – or of none. Some would say that standards are the central feature round which any quality system needs to be built. Others might say, more cautiously, that the publication of standards needs to come after a process of establishing what the organization is capable of and what is its public purpose. Certainly, the publication of standards (at least the kind that can be easily enforced through inspection and complaint) is yet another tool, among the many already identified, that can help towards greater clarity and explicitness.

However, standard-setting is – or should be – quite a risky process. Standards may appear to be a major challenge to well-established custom and practice; and in services dependent for their success on different parts of an organization, or on several different organizations, much greater levels of preparation and co-ordination may be needed than the present culture and structures allow before credible standards can even begin to be constructed. So there is always the risk that the publication of standards will not necessarily lead to better quality services: as we shall see, there is a great natural temptation to set standards that can definitely and easily be achieved, that is, to the lowest common denominator.

The debate is more complicated than at first it may seem. Several aspects need to be examined in this chapter. One essential question is whether such standards as do emerge are high, low or somewhere in between. Should they reflect current reality or are they an expression of intended future achievements? Are 'targets' the measurable aspect of what is achievable? How and by whom are they set? These issues form the first part of this chapter.

Then there is the question of language: the chapter will continue by looking at terminology. Are there significant differences between charters, promises, guarantees and citizen contracts, or are they different ways of expressing the same thing? Are there real distinctions in the underlying purposes of these different published pieces of paper? How might they be used? Who are they for, and what is the motivation of the organizations publishing them?

This analysis will lead to further questions, all germane to the quality debate. Depending on what they are to be used for – to create competition, to give rights of redress, to enable employees to know what is expected of them – the different ways of developing standards is significant. Who is involved in their development, how are they built up, is there a process – and motivation – to improve the standards once set? Values are, of course, at the back of this, and it is these same values that will help determine the relative importance (to service providers and to the public) of local and national standards. Values will also affect both the way different organizations choose to develop standards and even the choice of services among the multitude for which standards could hypothetically be developed.

At the same time, there are real tensions inherent in the development of standards, not unlike the tensions already analysed for the quality systems described in the last chapter. On the one hand, there is a pull towards standardization, towards making as few 'mistakes' as possible, to reach targets by whatever means, to avoid paying compensation. On the other, standards ought not to be static. There is a natural presumption that, once defined, standards will (or ought to) rise to meet rising expectations. New – and higher – standards are the concrete expression of the desire for continuous improvement. Like that process, they require willingness and ability to be flexible, to take risks or to encourage innovation.

Where do standards fit into the broad scheme of things? The national policy for Citizen's Charters promoted by central government merely involves one type of standard. We shall see that other approaches exist which may have more relevance to public services as a whole. However, the question needs to be asked whether, as with customer care, the notion of service standards stems from a philosophy that emphasizes individual consumers at the expense of consumer groups and of people in their role as citizens.

Finally, does standard-setting lead to better contract specification? How, if at all, does this process – the negotiation between purchaser and provider, between client and contractor – involve the public, whether as users or as citizens paying and voting for the service in question?

Ideal, attainable, minimum standards

Which services?

As Charlotte Williamson (1992) points out, it would be possible, given enough synergy between consumers' and professionals' interests, to devise measurable standards (that is, statements to which quantitative or qualitative measures can be attached) for most aspects of most services. The question is, which aspects of service – and which services – to cover, and what level to pitch the standard at? Both questions are laden with value judgments.

First, there is the question of coverage. The introduction of quality policies into an organization, particularly one that is still organized in traditional hierarchies and where work needs to be done on improving trust and communication between different tiers of management and staff can, as noted earlier, appear to devalue the past efforts of staff. They have been trying to deliver services adequately in the face of day-to-day constraints. The publication of standards, especially if they have not been involved in developing them, could seem a particular affront. Conversely, management, wishing to retain the loyalty of staff, may try to avoid some of the more difficult areas, even though these are the very ones that the public would wish to cover. Tensions between different groups of staff – between managers and professionals, for example –

could also lead to an avoidance strategy. Customer care type of standards may be published, as reception staff have little power, while the treatment of patients by doctors in their clinics, or the way that nurses respond to relatives' enquiries on hospital wards, may continue to be entirely dependent on the personal disposition of the individual concerned.

Another reason why aspects of service important to the public and to consumers are not covered by standards relates to the service chain. If front-line staff, with ultimate responsibility for delivering the service, are too far down the service chain, are too dependent on others and have too little control themselves, it could be pointless to devise a standard where the main result would be a stream of complaints and apologies.

At the time of writing (early 1994), two contrary examples of inappropriate standards were being publicized, one from the private sector, one from the public sector. First, pizza delivery firms were deliberately reducing their response (delivery) times: the desire for speed had led to too many road accidents. In contrast, the ambulance service unions were saying that the government-imposed response times, particularly in urban areas, were unrealistic because they did not allow for traffic conditions or staff shortages. In both cases, the use of response times as the basis for the target/standard was questionable: there were too many external factors they could not control. Other, less mechanistic but possibly less easily measurable indicators of quality could have been chosen, satisfactory both for the providers and for the consumers of the respective services, but perhaps needing changed ways of working, investment of new equipment, or simply more realistic information to the public.

Negotiating: what, with whom?

Ideally, the choice of service, or aspect of service, for which a standard is being devised would reflect something of the organization's values and the public's priorities. It is also an educational process, where the public, if it is allowed in on the act, has to become quickly familiar not only with the service itself, but also with the organizational culture and, perhaps, with professional ethics. So it might be better to start with services with which participants to the process have familiarity and for whom the service is important.

One of the early standards (1990) negotiated in Islington, for a local swimming pool, was able to build on the well developed participative process of the neighbourhood forum to identify local people's priorities and concerns about a service with which most people are quite familiar. Participants to the discussions could feel confident about the views they were expressing.

In Shipley (Bradford), a similar process of using a neighbourhood forum to discuss matters brought up by local people resulted in the involvement of traffic engineers in developing a standard (a service promise) for street lighting. Here, the public was asked to contribute to keeping up the standard by not only reporting lighting failures, but by noting the number of the streetlamp for easy identification. At the same time, it was necessary to warn the public both to report failures within defined hours and to be prepared for the promise not to be kept if the fault was traced to the regional electricity company. In other words, from the 'ideal' standard of being able to report street light failures at any time and to have them rectified, the 'realistic' or 'attainable' standard was negotiated that took account of office hours and of the service chain. A dialogue could be established where the views and needs of the practitioners and the local residents could be taken into account, debated and balanced with the many other factors such as budgets and resources, technical requirements, council priorities and the contribution that could be made by the public.

What was not negotiated was the kind of standard that said that 'x per cent of the lights will be working x per cent of the time'. This is a type of standard only too familiar to rail and underground passengers, where the caveats and restrictions are couched in such a way that the individual passenger on a single day has no way of knowing whether their late train is or is not inside the standard set. The charts displayed in the booking halls, pretty though they often are, serve as a further irritant, as the causes of failures are not published. It is easy to surmise, but difficult for passengers to prove, that the long-term lack of investment in the infrastructure means that the standards that they (we) really want – clean, comfortable trains that run on time – will never be available. It is in this context that the notion of standards loses its credibility.

However, in other areas of public service, indeed in those areas where the concept of Citizens' Charters first took shape – local government – a more thoughtful and honest approach has been possible. In York, where the first charter – 'customer contracts' – for environmental services such as street cleaning was published in 1989, the process was linked to market research, to public consultation about priorities and to an audit of present services. The aim, according to the Chief Executive, was not simply to describe existing services, but to list and target specific improvements within the following year (Wills 1991). These were reported on in the subsequent charter, as this was to be revised and published annually.

If we think of all the stakeholders and interests that might want a voice in defining a standard, it will be obvious that not everyone's wishes can be fulfilled. However, it may be helpful to think about what the service should be like in both the long and the short term. By doing this, it becomes possible to identify the real priorities of each group and, maybe, to agree a long-term aim (remembering that quality policies themselves take several years to implement). From there, shorter-term targets (in practice, the published standards) can be negotiated: the realities of legal, financial or political constraints can be balanced against what is possible and desirable. This is where the trade-offs in defining quality begin to operate – and where the need to redress imbalances of power is crucial.

In this way, a series of levels can be built up. First, there can be the ideal, perhaps five-year standard towards which the organization is publicly working. Second, there is the level that is being aimed at (better or more consistent than that already delivered, but achievable within statutory constraints and duties) within a set time period. And there is the basic minimum (sometimes enforceable by law) below which the service must not fall. It is the latter that tends to be the basis for compensation claims, where the organization thinks it is appropriate to pay them.

It is therefore worth looking for evidence of timescales and longer-term intentions, when reading the next service standard that comes with the gas bill, the council tax demand or, if you receive one, in the health authority newsletter. Is there any evidence of a long-term, ideal standard or a medium-term attainable standard, or does the document focus exclusively on minimum standards? Unfortunately, many of these documents are not dated, and have a tendency to hedge their bets. Thus an (undated) 'guarantee of service' (covering appointments, queries about bills, complaints and cut-offs of water supply) from Severn Trent Water states that even such 'guarantees' as are published are not legal documents and are not legally binding. (Customers are referred to the Water Supply and Sewerage Services (Customer Service Standards) Regulations 1989 – not published in the guarantee document.)

Comprehensiveness

Before leaving the question of what is or is not included in the standard for a service, it is worth reverting for a moment to the definitions of quality analysed in Chapter 3. The previous section was in some degree a reflection of the kind of definition that arises from different expectations and satisfaction rates – what do people want versus what will people put up with?

Depending on the type of service, it should also be possible to break down the contents of the service standard into the technical and non-technical components, into what the service is meant to do, and how (the interpersonal dimension) and where (the environmental dimension) it is to be achieved.

This division into three broad dimensions makes it easier to make explicit the fundamental nature of the service, and at the same time to avoid bland statements of a customer care nature that divert attention from the fact that the service itself may not be fit for the purpose. If, as they should be, standards are developed through a process of negotiation, then it is helpful if those involved know the ground rules. One of these must be the clarification of what can and cannot be discussed, and the reasons for it. The quality dimensions identified by Donabedian can help. They provide an agenda so that, for example, professional niceties can be challenged; or, in a less confrontational context, service providers can be given the opportunity, non-defensively, to explain the constraints under which they operate.

Standards, guarantees, charters and promises

Legal enforceability

If, as a citizen or as a fee-payer, taxes of some kind have paid for the service in question, then is an information leaflet, despite what the Severn Trent Water

Board stated in their 'guarantee' document, a legally binding implied contract? It tells citizens what is being done with their money and, presumably, if the information is explicit enough to be the basis of legal action, legal action could be taken if it turns out to be untrue. The annual reports and publication of Citizen's Charter indicators now legally required from local authorities possibly come into the same category. However, public service organizations could be tempted to try to avoid publishing any information, on the grounds that it could be actionable!

So it is probably better to proceed in the same spirit as some of those organizations currently publishing service standards: to demonstrate an intention to provide a high quality service; to inform the public about what to expect; and to give some grounds for redress of an unspecified (or sometimes specified) kind.

To make this work, the most important requirements (besides the internal quality management systems discussed in earlier chapters) are a working and credible complaints system and a reasonable level of public and employee goodwill. While goodwill and properly functioning complaints systems may be in short supply (hence the caution about developing standards too soon), they are not unthinkable. They are surely far preferable to a dependence on the courts and a huge and expensive bureaucracy dealing with compensation claims.

It is understandable that, particularly because of continued resource constraints, public service providers should be anxious not to raise expectations beyond the level where they can be met. But, given the right organizational climate and structure, it ought to be possible to develop standards, under whatever name, without the fear that identifying needs that could not be met would lead to litigation and conflict, for example under community care legislation.

Terminology

Are the different names attached to these documents significant? Some names may reflect a distinction between statutory (that is, required by Parliamentary statute or regulation) and other rights (enforceable through common, contract or constitutional law or only on the basis of goodwill). The following analysis of words used in a range of public documents is based on the common sense, everyday use of the words, turning to their legal origins only when absolutely necessary.

Rather obviously, any document headed 'Your *statutory rights*' comes into a category of its own, covering rights enforceable through the courts. Such statements should, of course, be generally available (though they may be difficult to keep up to date if there are frequent changes in the law), as well as being given to anyone whose statutory rights may need to be exercised or may be infringed at any time. Such statements are hardly part of a quality policy, though their production in clear, comprehensible language and their wider availability could come from broader thinking about quality and the publication of charters. They may be incorporated in wider-ranging documents. The Government's Council Tenants' Charter, for example, printed the rights of tenants embodied in law in red, the Government's view of what councils should do as a matter of good practice in blue and what the Government plans to do in the future in green.

Charters and *promises* are perhaps on the safest ground as regards to non-enforceability by law. They are merely a statement of intent and a source of information, in some cases (for example, York City Council's 1990–91 Citizen's Charter) reading remarkably like an election manifesto. There is, of course, an implied intention to fulfil the promise or charter (why publish it otherwise?), but the name itself gives no guarantee of redress. A charter can be very broad, expressing some fundamental principles but not going into detail. A 'promise' is likely to be more specific, relating to particular services. Both, however, are one-sided: the action is all on the side of the service provider, with nothing in the way of duties being spelt out for the service recipient or citizen. Nor would it be likely that they would provide the basis for formal redress. Their strength is in the published commitment to action, and in some cases (York again) in the willingness to publish the extent to which promises have or have not been fulfilled. Their credibility is likely partly to arise from the honesty of such statements – and the real improvements which may be emerging – and from a broader public assessment of the intentions and agenda of the organization over the whole range of its work (not just that covered by the charter or promise). Such promises depend on the efficacy of processes of public accountability, which in the current structure of public service can no longer be counted on (Stewart 1994).

The kind of charter described here is not, by the way, to be confused with the charter or petition, such as Charter 88, that sets out particular sets of rights that the signatories think citizens should have. It does not appear to confer any extra rights. Like many other examples of public language in recent years, the way words are used can mean almost the opposite of what a normal interpretation might lead people to expect!

Continuing the analysis of the language of quality standards, a public *contract*, unlike a charter or a promise, implies that there are at least two parties involved. Also, each party has rights as well as duties. Promises can be made unprompted and with no discussion expected or required. Contracts suggest a process of negotiation between at least two parties. They are therefore, in theory at least, stronger than charters or promises, codifying or actually increasing the rights to information and action for both users and citizens. (Such public contracts are, of course, different from client/contractor contracts linked to tendering processes, where all too often the public and users are excluded.)

Codes of practice (remember advertising and press standards) may be self-policing and voluntary, in which case they may have little validity, depending on the commitment of those involved. Or they may be enforceable or at least subject to external scrutiny. They may be formulated as a defensive reaction to external attacks (the Press) or past mistakes (child care), or they may provide another method of encapsulating on paper what the service is or is not intended to be. It is obviously important to know which kind of code is being presented and what rights can be derived from them, by the public and also by staff.

Codes of practice are mentioned here for completeness, rather than because they have been explicitly used (so far) as part of the new language of quality. However, they are obviously relevant to it. Like guarantees (see below), they are often hedged with conditions that contradict their apparent intentions, to the detriment of the consumers. Banking codes, for example, were found by the Banking Ombudsman to contain small print, much of which was 'written in language that was neither plain nor fair' (*The Guardian* 27 November 1993). The use by private sector providers of codes of practice as a guarantee of service – in home nursing care, for example – may look reassuring but is of equally doubtful validity when it comes to enforcement. Yet many Social Service Departments, which have rights to inspect residential care but have little or no control over private domiciliary services, are increasingly dependent on such firms, especially in holiday periods.

Service *guarantees* can be confusing if, like those produced by some of what used to be public utilities, they are hedged with statements of their non-enforceability in law. Much work has taken place in the field of consumer law to ensure that the small print of private manufacturers guarantees does not remove consumers' statutory rights. It would be a pity if, in the name of service quality, consumers were deterred in any way from exercising such rights.

Finally, quality *standards*, such as those of Devon County Social Services Department, may be published:

> Standards are statements which clearly and explicitly indicate what the key elements of a given service should be, the type of activity that should take place and the expectation of the way in which it should be delivered. . . . Standards can be about how much, or how well, or how often or how quickly something happens or something is done, and they may be expressed as percentages, numbers, frequency or cost.
>
> (Devon County Council 1993: 25)

As far as the Social Services Department of Devon County Council is concerned, the standards that are emerging have several different uses. These uses and perceived benefits are quite wide-ranging, in a way that the 'guarantees' and codes of practice or some of the other attempts to define the service may not be. They reflect both the philosophy to inform and empower service users and the process of organizational development, including the consultation with users and others, the use of clear language and avoidance of jargon, the intended triannual review and, once agreed, the mandatory nature of the agreed standards. For example, the standards are intended to:

● Provide a written reference point for users, carers, providers and policy makers (purchasers).

- Through the process of developing the standards, help to establish a vision of what the service should be.
- Provide a basis for assessing tenders for contracts.
- Provide a basis for locally negotiated service specifications.
- Help people decide what they mean by 'quality'.
- Provide a benchmark for assessment and review, to monitor current quality and help to plan future services.
- Help to resist pressure to reduce quality through cost savings.

There is a question of how the set standards (not negotiable and with no local variation) are to be implemented. Each standard – by 1993 they covered twelve different services such as care management, domiciliary personal care, family centres and so on – covers the aims and intended achievements of each service and, in some detail, what each person receiving the service can expect, under various headings such as information, competent staff, the process of the service itself and contract and monitoring methods. The expectation is that these standards will provide the tight part of a tight–loose framework for local managers to make their own decisions as to how to achieve the standards required. They are seen as the first step in a more complex process of evaluating services and where necessary establishing systems and models to support the quality policy.

This document has been quoted at length as an example of a carefully thought through approach to standard setting. However, even here, as the local managers would no doubt agree, there is some way to go between the construction of the standards and an assessment of their effect on the actual quality of the service received or available. The complications of the purchaser–provider split, the restructuring of the department to take account of this and of the community care and children's legislation, the need to build up new relationships with the health service and the voluntary and community sectors (see Smith *et al.* 1993), are all factors that make the apparently (fairly) simple task of constructing and measuring standards an extremely complex one in practice.

The purpose(s) of standard-setting

When it was introduced in 1991, the Government expected the Citizen's Charter to do two things (HMSO 1991). First, both in the Prime Minister's foreword and in the Introduction, 'standards' are introduced as one of the four main themes in the White paper (the others are quality – described as a programme for improving public services – choice and value): 'The citizen must be told what service standards are and be able to act where service is unacceptable' (HMSO 1991: 4). On the following page, under 'The principles of public service', is the following:

> Explicit standards, published and prominently displayed at the point of delivery. These standards should invariably include courtesy and helpful-ness from staff, accuracy in accordance with statutory entitlements, and a

commitment to prompt action, which might be expressed in terms of a target response or waiting time. If targets are to be stretched, it may not be possible to guarantee them in every case; minimum, as well as average, standards may be necessary. There should be a clear presumption that standards will be progressively improved as services become more efficient.

(HMSO 1991: 5)

This statement of principle about standards is one of several intended to underpin the Charter as seen by the Government. The other basic principles were: openness, information, choice, non-discrimination, accessibility and redress.

These principles were elaborated in the first report (HMSO 1992) where, together with a description of the twenty-eight national charters, the Government's preferred methods and mechanisms for improving services were reiterated. These were: measurement and inspection, regulation of privatized utilities, privatization and market testing (that is, compulsory competitive tendering for an increasing range of services formerly provided directly by public sector organizations) and devolved management in the form of 'Next Steps' agencies.

The underlying assumption is that market (or quasi-market) mechanisms will produce better services, that seeing how you compare with other service producers is a spur to improvement, and that redress is best achieved through individual complaints. This is a rather different philosophy from the one that prompted the first citizens' charters. These originated in local government – in York and Harlow to begin with – and were directed both towards meeting people's needs as willing or sometimes unwilling recipients of services, and to recognizing their rights as citizens.

The characteristics, strengths and weaknesses of the Prime Minister's 1991 Citizen's Charter have been fully analysed by others (Clifford 1993; Prior *et al.* 1993). The Government version of charters and standards has probably been a spur to making some service providers think about what the public needs to know about their services. It may also have stimulated consideration of what rights consumers and citizens have in relation to public (or recently privatized) services. This is particularly important for those services that have not yet begun to think in this way, though for others further down the road of quality improvements, it may simply be a diversion.

However, the reasons for developing standards needs to be clear. Do they arise naturally out of the values and objectives the organization has anyway been developing, are they integrated with mainstream policies? Or are they, like the nuclear industry's perfunctory bow towards environmental values, simply a cynical device to enable them to 'look good' (*The Guardian* 11 March 1994)? Hospital waiting lists and train timetables are two areas covered by the new charters where statistics can be massaged to make it appear that targets have been met. The public's actual experience of these services leads, not unreasonably, to a lack of confidence in the realities of charters. So charters must be credible if they are to be a useful tool in improving quality.

The question raised at the beginning of this chapter becomes more urgent. Are the various national and local organizations that provide public services only developing charters and quality standards because they feel they ought to or are being pressured into it by outside forces, notably the Government itself? If so, is there a danger that such activity may become a minimal response to the public's need for high quality services, with as short and precarious a life as some of the quality initiatives described in the last two chapters? Alternatively, can the introduction of a charter mentality stimulate the development of changes in the culture of the organization and its relationships with the public? It is striking that the first Citizen's Charter standards appear to have been devised purely as an internal affair, with no involvement of the public. Now there is interest and awareness that the public – generally in the role of users – does need to be involved if standards are to relate to real needs (HMSO 1992).

So the possible purposes of developing standards can be several. Some have already been quoted from the Social Services document from Devon and from the Citizen's Charter White Paper. Others may be less obvious, and may need to be extracted from between the lines of printed documents. Certainly, not all organizations publishing standards, promises, guarantees or charters will have the same aims, explicit or implied. What are these possible aims?

- Better information to the public.
- Empowering the public.
- Extension of individual consumer rights.
- Improving consistency, speed and overall quality of services.
- Providing the basis for inspection, measurement and regulation.
- Winning awards.
- Circumventing established employee rights (terms and conditions of service).
- Providing information to potential competitors.

A suspicious mind might find itself asking not only what is in the published standard, but what has been left out, and what are the caveats, again explicit or implied. It might want to know the policy context in which the standards have been developed. And, as suggested earlier, it might want to know why some services and not others have been chosen for the development of standards.

Much depends on the level of credibility of the organization and the commitment and sincerity with which the standards are implemented. Some of this credibility arises from knowledge of how the standards are constructed, especially the question of who was and is involved.

Who is involved in standard-setting?

It is rare but not impossible to find a statement within a published standard (or charter) that shows how the standard was arrived at and who was involved.

The use of neighbourhood forums and residents' associations has clearly been important in Bradford, Islington and Harlow. Consultation with users' and carers' organizations is part of Devon Social Services' policy for standard-setting. Swansea provides a tear-off slip inviting individual comments on its quality contracts for building control and housing benefits services.

For most of the documents collected by this writer, no such information is included. Bearing in mind the real difficulties of developing credible mechanisms for consultation and participation (Beresford and Croft 1993; Gaster and Taylor 1993), the involvement at a meaningful level of detail of community or consumers' representatives in the development of standards will be relatively rare. The question is, is there an intention to involve such groups, or are the standards and charters still producer-dominated?

The Citizen's Charter approach focuses on the relationship between the service provider and current, individual users. It is, as the Prime Minister put it in his Foreword, 'a testament of our belief in people's right to be informed and to choose for themselves'. Despite what is said in the preamble to the White Paper about non-discrimination, there seems to be little recognition either of the needs of those who do not, for a variety of reasons, currently use the services, or who do not exercise their rights in relation to them; or of the needs of people in their role as members of local communities and as collective citizens.

It is not only users (actual and potential) and the public whose needs have to influence the formulation of standards. The fashion for involving or consulting with users and/or the voluntary sector has tended to lead to the omission of front-line workers and trades unions. Whether this is deliberate or by default would depend on your view of the world. It is on them, of course, that the achievement of the standards depends. Yet in the novelty of discussing the details of services with consumers and local forums, there is a real danger that the rights and needs of workers, especially those in part-time, temporary and low paid jobs (overwhelmingly women) will be neglected (Foster and Crawley 1993). This is a point that is brought out in every single role play of standard-setting I have ever organized: the front-line worker feels isolated and powerless, the trade union representative begins to wonder what is happening to the rights won over the decades of the last century.

Role plays are artificial, but they illustrate graphically the need to recognize that the development of service standards is ideally a process of negotiation. No single group has an absolute right to have their needs met, if this is at the expense of others' needs. What is important is whose voice is heard – and listened to – and what weight is given to the different views and expectations that are bound to be expressed.

National and local standards; standards and standardization

The Charter programme will be pursued in a number of ways. The approach will vary from service to service in different parts of the United

Kingdom. The Citizen's Charter is not a blueprint which imposes a drab and uniform pattern on every service. It is a toolkit of initiatives and ideas to raise standards in the ways most appropriate to each service.

(HMSO 1991: 4)

While some national standards exist, through legislation or by the voluntary adoption of standards developed by the British Standards Institute or other accrediting bodies, they are not always appropriate to the particular circumstances in which specific services are being prepared and delivered. For example, despite the words quoted above, the Centre for Health Economics was concerned that the imposition of Government health targets could actually be producing less efficient services. Detailed, centrally set targets could not respond to local circumstances. Alternative ways of achieving the same results were not assessed, and targets did not appear to be based on any scientific evidence of what actions would produce the greatest 'health gain'. Greater benefits might be achieved by concentrating on different priorities (Jones 1991), according to knowledge of local needs and capabilities. It is in practice difficult to think of circumstances, other than where statutory rights are in question, where national standards for services ought to be developed except at a very high level of generality.

BS 5750, the quality assurance standard, was discussed in some detail in Chapter 5. It is, as was said there, a standard for assessing processes, not outcomes, and its applicability is limited because of that. However, despite the fact that it is a national standard, it is in fact more a framework for action and a set of principles to follow. A series of systems and procedures, covering different stages of production, has to be in place, but standard systems or procedures are not required. The philosophy is that different procedures will be relevant to different organizations.

The same principle could be applied to the development of service standards. First, their relevance and practicability within a particular organization (or part of an organization) at a particular time needs to be assessed. Then principles underlying the development of each standard need to be agreed: these would be consistent with the values and strategic objectives of the organization. Then the details of standards for individual services can be developed.

There may be some services, particularly the more routine ones, where considerable measures of standardization would be reasonable and desirable. These would be services where consistency and reliability are deemed to take preference over flexibility and responsiveness. But there are few services which do not contain some element of personal interaction – that is, after all, the definition of a service – and where, therefore, the requirements will differ from person to person or from community to community. Even in apparently very routine services, such as waste collection, the quality is likely to be perceived as far higher if attention is paid to the different needs of residents – the elderly, the disabled, or those living in remote areas for whom the dustmen (or women) may be the only visitors.

It may be easier to build such differentiation into a published standard for this type of universal service – identifying priority categories, for example, locating recycling schemes, or publicizing special help for removing large rubbish – than it is for the more personal services. There, flexibility is needed at the level of the individual and from day-to-day in a way that, whatever the variations, dust-cart drivers do not normally have to cope with. It is perhaps this kind of day-to-day variation that Devon Social Services means when they refer to the immutability of county-wide standards, while also expecting these same standards to provide the basis for local service specifications. There is a balance, in other words, between the tightness of a standard and the looseness of the way it is put into operation.

Maximum and minimum standards; the use of procedures and guidelines

Standards can be developed for different levels and types of activity. First, there is a basic *minimum* below which the service should not fall. Even this is easier to say than to do, as it is here that the greatest temptation lies for developing easily quantifiable, top-down and producer-dominated measures. Because these could in practice distort the service in a particular direction, qualitative indicators of how the basic minimum will be judged would be helpful. These minimum measures would need to apply across the board, at national, regional or local level. Their aim would be to ensure a broadly similar level of public expectation and a guarantee of fairness and reliability. They would, in other words, provide a safeguard for equity, building on existing practice to a considerable extent.

Second, there needs to be negotiation that, within the framework of a basic standard, can take account of local or particular needs and circumstances, looking towards a longer-term *ideal* standard. From this, *attainable* targets can be set, with time limits and measurable (qualitative and quantitative) achievements.

Third, there is the need for procedures to ensure standards are met. It would be impossible – and highly bureaucratic – to set separate standards for every anticipated activity. But there are almost certain to be some aspects of the service, some elements of the service chain, that can and should be the subject of procedures. The aim would again be to ensure consistency and fairness and, ultimately, accountability. Procedures are not the same as standards, because they are internal administrative matters designed to ensure that policy is carried out; but they are closely related to standards, and are – through Ombudspersons, the Audit Commission and other inspectorates – subject to scrutiny on behalf of, if not by the public.

The fourth element in establishing service standards, especially for non-routine services where high levels of personal discretion is exercised, could be the provision of published policy frameworks and guidelines against which specific decisions can be checked. These guidelines would help the development of the devolved management, identified in the last chapter as almost a *sine qua non* for effective quality systems.

Measuring standards and targets: incentives for action

Standards exist, whether they are good enough, or whether they are put into writing or not. But in moving from the implied to the explicit, and in aspiring to improve existing standards, or make them more consistent, choices exist. These choices include such issues as what services and aspects of service to cover, what rights may be inferred or given by published standards, what involvement there might be in their formulation, both of the public (consumers *and* citizens) and of staff. What is the point of putting a lot of effort into developing public standards?

Rewards and incentives

If it is believed that people will not act unless they are financially rewarded (through performance-related pay or special awards) or threatened (through competition), then standards and the targets derived from them would need to be measurable in such a way that quite precise assessments of achievement could be made. The Government's use of league tables in many areas of public service, and the notion of devolving performance-related pay decisions right down the management hierarchy, are both reflections of this ideology.

If, however, the underlying assumption is that staff are motivated to give a good service because they have an altruistic belief in the idea of public service, then increased job satisfaction – knowing you have the support to do the job well – will be the main incentive. In that case, qualitative public and management feedback will be a far more effective spur to action than a financial bonus arising from the fact that all telephone calls have been answered within three rings, or that letters have been responded to within a set number of days.

It is noteworthy that not a single quality guru, even though they are generally discussing the market-oriented private sector and the incentive of developing a competitive edge in the outside world, advocates systems of individualistic, pay-related employee rewards. Instead they emphasize the role of teams, the ethos of co-operation and the rewards of team membership. The satisfaction of knowing that suggestions for improvements will be listened to and taken up where appropriate, of feeling valued and trusted are, in this philosophy far more important and effective than systems which, by rewarding individuals, create internal competition and divisiveness.

As far as the public is concerned, standard-setting may be a useful way of ensuring financial redress if things go wrong. Treating people as customers leads to a money-back mentality: if the customer (or passenger, or water user) finds out how to claim, they can get financial compensation or its equivalent in vouchers. For those public services that most closely resemble private sector services, this may be acceptable. However, given the choice, many 'customers', and certainly those members of the public denied compensation because of the complicated rules, or who retain a notion of public services being for the general good, would prefer a different kind of response. They would prefer organizations to demonstrate an intention to learn from mistakes, rather than paying people to keep quiet.

Those standards that have been developed in consultation with the public tend to have these broader considerations in mind. Their ethic is not to identify (and close loopholes to) grounds for compensation to disgruntled 'customers', but to acknowledge the public purposes of public services, and to show understanding that in many cases, especially in relation to rationed or compulsory services, compensation would both be inappropriate and irrelevant. Taxpayers do not want to pay for things twice. And the very nature of a service (it cannot be replaced or sent back to the manufacturer for rectification) means that a real effort to put things right would be more helpful to the recipient and to future recipients than any apology or voucher.

For this kind of approach to redress, statements of rights and duties, of grounds for complaint, and of systems of audit and inspection are likely to be more important both for producers and the public than the more quantitative approach often going under the name of quality. Complaints systems can be used as a management tool (Atkins 1992), and may be seen as positive contributions to service improvements, while quantitative targets can actually distort service priorities. We shall return to this issue in the next chapter.

Standards and contracts

Research for the Department of the Environment by the Institute of Local Government Studies (Walsh and Davis 1993) examined the effects of the 1988 Local Government Act on the way clients and contractors were behaving. When looking at quality issues, several points were noted in connection with the development of service standards. These are some of the findings:

- It was difficult to set standards because of the lack of previous experience, the lack of suitable data and the difficulty of expressing the subjective elements of a service in the form of a standard.
- The standards that were set tended to be more consistent than previously, but had proved to be no guarantee against patchy performance, especially in areas of work with high staff turnover, new techniques and lack of training (building cleaning, for example); or the tender had been underpriced, presumably in an effort to win the contract in the first place, leading to skimpy work.
- There was a tendency to work to minimum standards.
- Some of the standards set were lower than those achieved previous to competition, especially where programmes of service improvements were already in place.

The lessons from this research have considerable resonance. Some benefits appear to be emerging from the process of standard-setting and contract formulation. However, these need to be set against the concerns raised by the temptation to set minimum (low?) standards that are easily achievable and may even be worse than before.

At the same time, there is no evidence that the public is involved in this highly bureaucratic process at any stage, although evidence from other research and action (Gaster, forthcoming; Gaster and Taylor 1993; Harrison 1993; Norah Fry Research Centre 1990) shows that is it possible to involve local groups in the development of contract specifications and of local standards.

Conclusions

Before writing this chapter, I thought that the publication of almost anything that would help the public to know more about and have the tools to challenge the full range of public services must be a 'good thing'. Even the least satisfactory and most tokenistic standards, I thought (in my role as a member of the public), would provide a footing from which further progress could be made towards real improvements that would benefit staff and public alike.

It now seems to me that a rather careful and cautious approach is necessary. The use of language, apparently couched in everyday terms but, on examination, open to a range of interpretations some of which, like 'guarantee', 'charter' or 'contract', may even contradict the normal use of the word, can be misleading. The failure to involve consumers, residents or staff in the construction of standards undermines their credibility and probably their effectiveness. The assumptions about human behaviour that seem to underlie an emphasis on individual performance, on individual consumers and on quantitative measurements, are possibly (and probably) in actual contradiction to the notions underlying quality policies and implementation programmes. They work against a quality culture that requires collective, collaborative and co-operative approaches to service provision.

The other side of the coin is that the development of standards, charters, promises or guarantees has led the service providers to think more clearly about the nature of the service, to define priorities and, in some cases, to consult or obtain feedback from the public in a way that would not have happened before. While such charters and standards do not appear to confer any more rights than existed previously, they do perhaps convey a moral obligation to be more answerable and responsive to the public.

If asked whether the development of standards is essential to an effective quality policy, the answer would almost certainly be 'yes'. But it is important to be clear that they are not simple to construct and maintain. They are not objective, any more than are the definitions of quality analysed in Chapter 3. And developing a standard is merely the beginning (or the middle) of a long process.

Standards, by whatever name they are known, are certainly not a substitute for a properly thought out quality policy. They can, however, be important symbols and tools of just such a policy.

7

Measuring, monitoring, evaluating

Telling the difference between a good service and a bad service

Is measurement possible?

Over the last four years, I have accumulated two piles of documents about measuring quality. One pile consists of articles and reports about the process of performance measurement: here, quite rightly, many of the very real difficulties of collecting and using appropriate data and information are identified. The other pile is a set of papers, published and unpublished, reporting attempts to measure quality in particular services. These are generally fascinating documents, because they show how the detail of public services may be assessed in a way that could (should?) have a real effect on the quality of the service in question. Different methods are tried – consumer surveys, observation, audits, consumer panels, focus groups, priority search, data returns, mystery customers – which add up to a useful set of techniques, and an indication of the variety and combination of approaches that managers seriously interested in improving quality could try out.

Oddly enough, league tables are not mentioned: perhaps this reflects the bias of my very unrepresentative sample of papers (generally obtained in connection with front-line activities), perhaps their absence reflects the unease with which most practitioners view them.

There is a problem, with the mountain of material now available about measuring and monitoring services, about what to include in a book of this nature. Thinking about this, I asked a social worker what he thought about measuring quality. The first thing, he said, was to know what consumers think of your service. How would you go about this? Can you ask people, often powerless recipients of the very service you are asking questions about, to say what they really feel? Are all consumers capable of answering – incapacity or even death will rule some out, especially if, in order to overcome the power and dependence issues, you wait until after the service is complete. Who should ask the questions – the service provider, peers, external assessors, other users? Will the replies be accurate and honest? How will they be used?

Is it all too difficult to contemplate? No, he thought: it *is* important to know the difference between a good service and a bad service. Some attempt at measuring results is the only way of doing this.

The Audit Commission, coming at the same issue from a rather different angle, feels (like this social worker), that just because no performance measurement system is perfect and measuring quality hardly tried, that is not a reason for not doing it:

> The Commission therefore believes that it is a disservice to local government to dwell too much on the theoretical difficulties of measuring performance. What is more useful is to propose practical ways in which local authorities actually can measure their performance, while avoiding the worst consequences of misleading indicators.
>
> (Audit Commission 1989: para. 17)

So the rest of this chapter will try to concentrate on the practical issues of measurement and on the choices managers at all levels can make so as to avoid the pitfalls and create positive, if limited, achievements. There are parallels here with the earlier discussion of ideal, practicable and minimum standards: bearing in mind costs and other practical and technical constraints, there will generally be a gap between what is desirable if all aspects of quality were to be measured, and the reality of what, within existing resources and levels of commitment and involvement of key parties, can actually be achieved.

Where does measurement and monitoring fit into a quality policy?

Monitoring and measurement are, in a way, both the end-point and the starting point for developing and putting into practice a policy for improving service quality. Measurement – qualitative, of course, as well as quantitative – is the only way of obtaining information on what services are being provided and how they are being received and perceived (Nicholson 1993). So measurements, in the form of public survey data, management information systems data, verbal and written feedback from staff, consumers and the public, can both contribute to providing a benchmark and an audit of what is currently happening, and can provide the basis for assessing whether particular objectives or specific targets are being achieved. Going back to the model presented in

Chapter 1, measuring, monitoring and assessment of quality can take place at three stages: diagnosis, implementation (as part of the problem-solving process) and as the basis for evaluation and planning the next phase.

What measurement cannot do on its own is to improve quality. It needs to be part of a policy and a culture that welcomes and uses the results of measurement to assess and develop the level and type of quality required by the organization's values and objectives. In isolation, especially if imposed from outside, measurement can often be seen as a threat, something to fear or to manipulate to the best advantage. It is not seen as a way of helping service deliverers improve their services, but as a way of defending the providers' position.

As with other aspects of implementation systems, the choice of what, how and when to measure, insofar as it rests within the organization, needs to be consistent with the policies, attitudes and behaviour that govern the service delivery for which the organization is directly or indirectly responsible. The discussion in the last chapter showed that standards developed without the input of those most concerned, especially if their achievement is also the basis of decisions about performance related pay or other individualistic rewards, will not necessarily contribute to a balanced development of overall quality, nor will they necessarily benefit the public.

The Stakhanovite norms being imposed on many public services by Central Government, together with insecurity of employment, short-term contracts and staff cuts are unlikely to improve staff morale. Why should staff contribute to measuring what might be their own demise? If measurements must be produced, at least let them be in the workers' favour. Alec Nove (1993) quoted the Soviet academics who, because they would be penalized for student failures, hardly failed anyone. In the time and motion studies of the 1950s and 1960s, workers would consciously slow down their rate of production to ensure that the norms for the next round of pay and bonuses were reasonably easily achievable. The quality would inevitably sink to the lowest and slowest.

The current widespread use of performance measures as instruments of punishment and external judgment, rather than as tools for development, has much the same flavour. Accountability and a willingness to be assessed is an important part of public service, but the 'evaluative state' (Henkel 1991), with its world of inspectors, assessors and regulators, has a grim sound of centralized control that seems to have little to do with service quality, whatever the good intentions of individual agencies and officers.

There is no need to pursue this theme further. The issue is that, if it is to be meaningful, performance measurement for quality, in the particular climate within which most public service workers now operate, needs to have very clear benefits: to staff, to the public and to the organization. It needs to be closely connected with and relevant to everyday tasks, and the results have to be available in a form that is useful, comprehensible and timely. Data can be aggregated or disaggregated for different uses, put together in such a way that like can be compared with like (over space and time), packaged with other sources of information to convey a rounded picture, and be usable for different purposes and by different stakeholders. But if they are not useful to front-line and back-line managers, to workers, consumers and the public at large, they will be subject to the same levels of suspicion, the same avoidance tactics, and the same manipulation as has so often been reported for the measures of quantity that already dominate performance measurement (Bouckaert 1990; Carter 1988, 1991; Gaster 1991b; Pollitt 1988).

Issues in measuring quality

Quality measurement having, I hope, been firmly located within a broader framework of policies, values and objectives, what are the issues of principle and practice facing public service managers? The following list may not be comprehensive, but as a starting point for thinking, it may be of some use. Discussion of each main issue takes up the remainder of this chapter:

- *What types of measure should be used?* Any kind of measure, quantitative or qualitative, needs to be reasonably reliable and valid, but there may be different ways of assessing this. A choice also exists between looking for surrogate indicators of quality, and/or explicitly accepting/welcoming qualitative indicators, based on attitudes and perceptions. Other criteria, especially that of 'relevance' could also affect the choice of measure or indicator.
- *Who needs to be involved?* This question that has permeated the book, and was covered at length in Chapter 2. Nevertheless, it is worth reiterating the role of the public and of front-line staff in a world where measurements, while purportedly for their benefit, seem so often to pass them by.
- *What is being measured?* The focus of measurement ought to relate intimately to the definition(s) of quality adopted, and to strategic objectives. At the same time, there is always a danger of measurement overload – the temptation to measure anything that moves; or of imbalance – the power of certain groups to avoid or evade measurement of their work.
- *How will the measurements be used?* Do different purposes affect what to measure and how to do it? Will different answers be given according to how respondents think their information will affect people delivering the service?
- Whether the indicators are qualitative or quantitative, there are many *different ways of collecting data*. Bearing in mind organizational values, particularly those affecting the relationships with the public and the value placed on staff, are some methods more appropriate than others for the measurement of quality? Can or should a mixture of methods be employed?
- *When should measurement take place?* This is worth separate consideration. One of the most common objections to measurement is that it is not timely – the policy has not had time to be implemented, problems have been encountered, new staff have been taken on board and so on. And, on the other side of the coin, pressure for results, from politicians or from the public, may lead to judgments of success being made too soon, failing to take

account of the relatively long timescales needed for implementing quality policies.

- Finally, a question that links back to standards and objectives is, *what criteria* are used to judge whether the data collected shows an improvement in service quality? Do these criteria change, for example as expectations and standards rise over time?

To some extent, these questions are interdependent. If it is thought, for example, that senior managers are the only people who need to decide what is to be measured and how the data is to be used (a common situation in local government), the methods and types of measure will be those that assist the kinds of decision senior managers have to make: the allocation of resources, the determination of service priorities. In this case, management information systems designed to measure economy and efficiency, with perhaps some public opinion surveys to legitimate service priority decisions, are the most likely.

On the other hand, if front-line staff, like the social worker quoted earlier, want feedback about their services so that they can focus their efforts more effectively and, preferably, provide a 'better', more satisfactory service, then there might be more emphasis on qualitative measures, on the use of more continuous, consultative methods, on using the information as the starting point for a process of self-evaluation and action planning.

If it was up to the public to decide how to measure the quality of particular services, the aim might be to produce data and information that would provide ammunition for asking challenging (and/or helpful) questions of the service providers, and to join the debate about service priorities and standards.

This range of different needs, generating different data, matches – imperfectly because of overlapping interests – the points on the quality cycle where measurement can take place. Senior managers and politicians want diagnostic and summative data, enabling judgments to be made. Front-line workers and managers want formative data that will improve day-to-day decisions and the process of implementation. The public is interested both in the day to day and in the more strategic aspects of quality and will want a say, assuming organizational values and a culture that allows this, at different stages and in different ways throughout the cycle.

What types of measure should be used?

The actual measures that could be used to assess quality will be discussed later. But there are different ways of looking at data. These affect the choice of what and how to measure, and indeed whom to involve. So, although most of this discussion is of the chicken and egg kind – each decision is to a greater or lesser extent dependent on something else – the general approach to measurement is quite a good starting point.

The first question is whether quantitative measures are somehow more objective than qualitative measures. The answer is, I think, that there is little to choose between them. The key question is not 'can this be converted to (preferably statistically valid) figures?' but 'does it in fact measure what we think it is important to measure?'

Christopher Pollitt, discussing the role consumers (broadly defined) might have in the measurement of quality, pointed out that an accountancy approach to measurement focuses on the costs and benefits of the immediate service transaction. It does not take into account the externalities affecting a much broader section of society than simply the immediate user or provider (Pollitt 1988). Measurement of quality needs to take account of this, often by canvassing opinion and looking far more widely than apparently simple and uncontestable statistical returns of input or throughput (the most common type) or output. Carers, neighbours, families and communities are all affected, yet consumer surveys and headcounts concentrate only on current users.

Different kinds of measurement are needed, and these will tend to be of the qualitative type, involving assessments of opinion, attitudes and experience in a way that cannot necessarily be captured by sets of hard data. Hard data is in any case generally considerably less hard or objective than at first appears as behind each set of data, choices are made about what to measure and what not to measure, how to measure and how to present the results. These measures are based on a value judgment of what is important, acceptable, relevant and presentable.

The main weakness of the quantitative data method is that of the 'measurable driving out the non-measurable' (Bovaird 1975): only those aspects of a service that can be counted are measured. These may not be the most important ones, especially in the eyes of consumers; consequently, numerical measurements are never comprehensive. This reduces their validity, their relevance. What is extraordinary is how long this has been known and acknowledged and yet how easy it still is for so-called objective data to be presented as if it were the truth.

However, the question of validity and reliability affects all types of measurement, qualitative possibly even more than quantitative. It is the fear that qualitative methods are not reliable and valid in a way that quantitative methods claim to be that can inhibit their use. In practice, as both the long years of opinion polling since the 1930s and recent developments in the measurement of quality itself show (Parasuraman et al. 1988b), items included in opinion research, and the scales attached to them can be tested for both reliability (do they produce consistent results?) and validity (do they measure what they purport to measure?).

Some of these forms of measurement are transferable to the measurement of public service quality (see Speller (1992) and Gosschalk (1989) discussing MORI public opinion polls). Mixed qualitative/quantitative instruments are, therefore, available to the public services. Qualitative questions can be asked, and quantitative results produced.

However, a qualitative approach involves more than opinion polls. There can be a dialogue between providers and the public, in the form of panels and focus groups, observations and audits, ongoing consultation methods and quality action groups. Internally, diagnostic problem-solving techniques can be used to find out existing levels of quality, the location of weak points and the desirability of different options for actions. All these techniques explicitly and overtly depend on human judgments, and for those who feel safer with the apparently objective figures produced by data returns or opinion polls, such methods may seem suspect: managers worry about reliability; the results can be rubbished by those who do not like them.

One way round this problem is to use several different techniques to assess the quality of the same service. This triangulation method is familiar to researchers using qualitative methods. By interviewing or observing different groups of 'actors', a series of perspectives can be obtained and compared, giving credibility to the findings. Such findings can also be integrated with those produced by regular (or one-off) statistical data, again for the purpose of cross-checking and assurance of reliability.

The validity question is slightly different. This is the issue of ensuring that the 'right' questions get asked in the first place. In this new field of measurement experiments are needed, and there will inevitably be a certain amount of trial and error. However, I can suggest two tests of validity, or relevance. Both involve examining the actions that result from the findings, though of course it is not always possible to be sure of the connection between cause and effect.

First, does the choice of indicator and measurement methods affect the behaviour of service providers, distorting the service towards fulfilling these measures at the expense of other aspects of the service? Is, for example, thoroughness being sacrificed – or traded off – for speed (Burningham 1992)? Are some groups being creamed off for service at the expense of others who need more time and energy and are therefore less attractive to those trying to fulfil their norms (Propper 1992; Employment Department 1994). Is behaviour being changed to meet the needs of the statistics, not the consumer (Nove 1993)?

Second, and more positively, do the findings of qualitative (and quantitative) sources of feedback appear to be having a positive effect on the service? Do they make sense to those who need to use the findings in a practical way, at whatever level in the organization or outside it? Does evaluation and action planning that actually improves services arise from the findings of these measurements? If so, this gives them their own validity – they are seen to be useful!

There will never be perfect ways of measuring quality. The aim here has been to discuss how one might choose between different methods. Measurement can be difficult, expensive and time-consuming. It is worth feeling confident that the effort and the results will bring some benefits – and will not, conversely, actually lower the quality of the service in a way that an exclusive dependence on statistically reliable quantitative measurements might do.

Having said all this about reliability and validity, the most important criterion to apply to the choice of measures and methods may be that of ownership. Resistance to measurement, and rejection of the findings, are all too easy if no part has been played in devising and choosing the measures, or if the results are fed back in a judgmental rather than constructive way. Top-down or externally imposed measures may be needed to help the fair allocation of resources or for other overt management and political purposes. But it is not sensible to pretend that they are appropriate for the measurement of quality. Quality has to be produced by those working in organizations, and received or perceived by the public. Its measurement must logically be an integral part of the overall quality framework.

Who needs to be involved?

If measurement and assessment is to have a constructive influence on the quality of public services, it seems obvious that front-line staff, consumers and the public should be involved in each of the processes that together produce a measurement system. It can be helpful to have access to the fresh eye or comparative perspective brought by an external evaluator. But even this process may well be useless and ineffective if there has been no consultation with or involvement of those whose work is being assessed.

Each group involved in measurement needs to have the opportunity to think about: (1) the purpose of measurement in relation to service and quality objectives; (2) coverage; (3) methods; (4) timing; (5) time taken and costs; and (6) how the information is to be used.

Thought needs to be given to whether the same data can be used for different purposes, whether summary or simplified reports are needed, whether there should be translations or other methods of communication, feedback meetings and discussions. What right do those who have gathered the data (staff, consumers, 'experts', inspectors, etc.) have to interpret and present it? Does anyone have the right to suppress findings (would this be consistent with a policy for quality?). Has full consideration been given to confidentiality and other ethical issues? And so on.

The basic argument is for a more 'bottom-up' approach to the measurement of quality than is currently apparent in the way performance measures and indicators are being used to measure what the public services are doing. It is a further argument for a new kind of organizational culture that acknowledges the key role of front-line staff and the public in the overall development of quality in the public services and creates a climate of feedback and constructive criticism.

What is being measured?

Chapter 3 drew on a variety of sources and experience in an attempt to define quality. Self-evidently (I think), quality cannot be measured until it has been defined, however loosely. So any programme of monitoring and evaluation needs ideally to start with a process of clarifying the nature and objectives of the service, in the context of organizational values such as equity, equality, greenness, centralist/decentralist, building new forms of democracy and accountability, honesty or whatever, including the pursuit of economy, efficiency or effectiveness.

Dimensions of quality and consumer satisfaction

The definitions that are agreed are likely to fall into several broad groups. Within each group, there will be a set of characteristics. Parasuraman *et al.*, for example, identified through their initial research (1988a) ten main dimensions of quality. They then developed a list of 97 items on a seven-point scale to test public expectations. After testing and subsequent refinement, the list was eventually collapsed into a 22-item, five dimensional scale called SERVQUAL.

The five final SERVQUAL dimensions were: (1) tangibles (the equivalent of the environment/ambience dimension of Donabedian and Stewart and Walsh); (2) reliability (equivalent to the technical dimension); (3) responsiveness; (4) assurance; and (5) empathy (all part of the non-technical, interface dimension).

The authors note that this instrument, a market research device, would be useful in measuring the relative importance of different factors in different types of service. It was, they claimed, applicable over a wide range of (private sector) services. However, they also thought that, if the overall quality of the service was to be thoroughly tested, it should be used in conjunction with other types of measure such as employee surveys.

The SERVQUAL scale simultaneously builds on two crucial aspects of service quality. These are:

- That quality is a collection of characteristics, which differ in their relative importance in different services.
- That quality can, once the key characteristics have been identified, be at least partly measured through customer (consumer) satisfaction, this being calculated as the difference between expectations (of a service in general) and perceptions/experience (of a particular version of the service).

The SERVQUAL instrument assumes that the service being measured has been chosen by the customer. Different items might have to be found to illustrate key dimensions of public services. For example, items would be needed to take into account issues of accountability and equity and the fact that very few such services can be 'chosen' by their consumers. The use of an instrument such as this could also be extended to test citizen attitudes and perceptions. But SERVQUAL is certainly less blunt than many of the public opinion/satisfaction surveys currently used to test attitudes to public services, and the results can help managers and the public pin down more precisely what improvements are needed.

Trade-offs and measurement in relation to 'standards'

Such surveys would not be the only way of measuring the perceived characteristics of each service (see below, under Methods). David Burningham, in his very thorough analysis of performance indicators (PIs) from an economist's perspective is clear not only that trade-offs between different characteristics take place in practice, but also that the ideal trade-off – that is, the actual level (standard) of quality intended – will be the outcome of a combination of factors subject to explicit or implied negotiation. This trade-off reflects the perceptions and priorities of the range of interests that would be involved; it might also be a compromise between various (possibly conflicting) organizational values that affect the choice of key characteristics, particularly in multi-disciplinary services.

Burningham (1992) draws attention to the large amount of data currently being collected (he refers to local government, but the same is true of the health service). Much of this is not useful for measuring quality and its collection actually distorts service priorities to the probable detriment of the service. Depressingly, Burningham found that out of an average 400 performance indicators used (across all departments) by nine local authorities, only 21 per cent could be described as performance measures (defined as 'more comprehensive measures of performance', covering all the relevant dimensions of the service in question). All the other indicators were management statistics – statements of quantity that do not measure performance (numbers of clients for example); and partial indicators, whose meaning on their own is often ambiguous: what are unit costs actually measuring?

Inputs, throughputs, outputs and outcomes

Some of these indicators could nevertheless be useful. Measures of what goes into a service as well as measures of the process of service are desirable as a check on the quality of inputs and throughputs, identified earlier in Chapter 3 as aspects of quality that need to be considered and defined.

For example, for a service to be of high quality, the resources – the training and experience of staff, the information to the public about the services, the communication system between departments – also need to be of high quality. Put into context, some management information systems or internal surveys established for other reasons could be channelled to provide the necessary information. Expenditure on services is also generally seen as an input: this is probably the information that is most readily available, even though it is meaningless if divorced from information about what the service actually does (throughputs and outputs).

Throughputs are the aspect of service most commonly measured through existing performance indicators. It is here that quantitative indicators are particularly prominent and insidious. The most common type of indicator is the headcount. If, as in the health service, this is a major criterion for decisions on pay and promotion or for the retention of contracts, there is a strong incentive to move people quickly through the system or, because of the way the figures are counted, pass them to other departments (thereby losing continuity and co-ordination). The quality perceived by patients – and probably by health staff too – must suffer. Yet it may be in defiance of the system, a risk not worth running, to keep a patient in hospital a little longer, so as to try to prevent an early return through relapse or lack of social care.

This point was illustrated graphically recently when, in the course of research on collaboration in community care (Smith *et al.* 1993), I naïvely asked what were 'FCEs' and why were they important. It turned out, for those who do not know (the language may have changed by now) that these were 'finished consultant episodes' ('death or discharge' in former terminology) and were the basis of payment to potential providers of health care. Turnover, not results, was the thing. (This is not to say that as many people as possible should not be treated. It is the inappropriate use of performance indicators as the driving force in discharge decisions, and the fear that too little priority may be given to liaison and co-ordination, that is the point of concern.)

In a very different context, the pressure for high throughputs, again as the basis for performance targets, was found by the chief adjudication officer for social security payments (*The Guardian*, 26 November 1993) to be leading directly to huge numbers of payment errors (the focus here was on overpayments). This resulted in inconvenience to claimants involved through no fault of their own in recovery proceedings, and huge losses (not counting the staff cost of re-work) for taxpayers. Accuracy was being sacrificed for speed and the numbers game.

The current dominance of this kind of measure should not, however, prevent a search for measures that relate to the quality of the throughput – of what happens to people once they are in the system. It is, in any case, as was pointed out in the discussion of technical and non-technical dimensions of quality, sometimes hard to distinguish between throughput/process and output in a service, as the output is also the very process of being served – the interpersonal factors of the service relationship.

While immediate outputs of a service – was an operation done, a child taken into care, a homeless person housed (or not) – can be measured quite easily in terms of numbers, the quality is more difficult to assess. Was it the right operation, done with maximum sensitivity? Was it right to take the child into care, and were parents and relatives, and the child itself, involved in the decision? Was the homeless person dumped in a 'sink' estate, or, within constraints, were needs and resources carefully matched?

If measuring the quality of outputs is difficult, it is even more of a problem with regard to outcomes. How can the achievement of strategic quality objectives, or effectiveness, be assessed? Part of the difficulty is in specifying what the expected or intended outcome might be. Is it improved quality of life and, if so, how is *that* measured? (The demise of the Oregon experiment where public opinion was canvassed about the health conditions that should get priority treatment – resulting almost inevitably in the prospect of giving automatic priority to premature babies over hip replacements – has, I hope, put paid to the notion of quality of life indicators, or QALYs, as the basis of what medical care to provide, if any.) Is it that people got what they wanted? Would councillors see it in terms of improved turnouts at elections? Would professionals judge quality effectiveness in relation to the achievement of their professional expectations of what they were trained to do?

Part of the difficulty is to distinguish the contribution of a particular service to an overall situation where many other factors, including the placebo effect, may have been at work. A further question is, when is an outcome an outcome? How much time needs to elapse before the effect of a service can be judged? Yet it is this, in the end, that could be taken as the key test of quality.

Measurement of quality outcomes (as opposed to policy outcomes) may even continue to be too difficult and problematic for the moment. This may seem defeatist, but with a field as broad and untried as that of measuring quality, there is plenty of ground to cover that is practicable and, as the Audit Commission suggested for its Citizen's Charter indicators (1992), acceptable – to citizens, local authorities, service professionals and other interested parties. *Not* in the first instance to try to measure outcomes and effectiveness in relation to service quality could be a conscious choice that managers may want to make.

How will the measurements be used?

Managers wishing to measure the quality of their services could ask themselves two rather different questions. These are:

- What do I need to know so as to make sure the service is being delivered to the correct specification or standard? (The accountability and control question.)
- What do I need to know so that the service quality can be improved? (The development question.)

The first question assumes that standards exist and are specified closely enough to be measured. It implies that judgments will be made, to ensure that the ethos of public service and accountability is upheld or as the basis for reward or punishment.

Information may be given to senior managers, politicians or official inspectors/evaluators. It may be used to determine future policy priorities and resource allocation, for deciding how best to develop services for the under-fives, for example (Webster 1990), or to make a judgment about whether to continue or develop a pilot approach or project (Gaster *et al.* 1992).

The second question may arise from an existing standard, but could equally be part of an initial diagnosis, a benchmarking process against which to measure future progress: it sees information as part of a developmental, formative process, as a starting point for further work. In this case, the information will be fed back to staff and, if they are involved in the quality policy, to consumers and the public. It will be used to raise questions, identify areas of variance (over place and time) that need to be examined in more detail, and provide the basis for a detailed programme of action.

Data collected for management information systems is very often not fed back to the staff who collected it. It becomes part of the tension between the front line and senior management, or between professionals and managers, increasing rather than reducing the distance between them. It is a 'game', played to increase resources, to keep management quiet, to maximize personal rewards, to win or retain contracts. It is manipulative rather than constructive. Similarly, the results of public opinion surveys, or external consultants' reports may remain confidential, perhaps because of the not unreasonable fear that negative findings will be misinterpreted out of context. However, this attitude is often a reflection of a culture that does not value or trust staff, and where internal communications are poor.

It is even more rare for service data to be given to members of the public, whether as users or as citizens (Pollitt 1988), though access to personal data is now possible. The first rung on the 'ladder of participation' (Gaster and Taylor 1993) is access to information. On the assumption that a quality policy must involve public and staff, then making the results of quality measurements available, to inform consultation and participation, is probably crucial to the overall effectiveness of the policy.

Quantitative and qualitative quality measurements can, then, be used in several ways, summatively (to make a judgment) or formatively (as part of a learning process). These are:

- To decide whether standards are being met.
- To provide a baseline for judging the current level of quality.
- To make comparisons between similar organizations or from year to year (the units of comparison and methods of data collection may differ and care needs to be taken that the data is indeed comparable).
- To enable the organization to win contracts or obtain funding both by demonstrating what it does and by exhibiting a willingness to be evaluated.
- As feedback to service providers; as an incentive for improvement (whether or not tied to individual or collective performance targets and/or pay).
- As a developmental and learning tool, to help decide where improvements need to be made.
- As an aid to empowering public and staff (information is power – if not doctored and if presented in acceptable and accessible forms).

These purposes, or uses of quality measurements are not mutually exclusive. Indeed, it would be reasonable to expect that organizations providing public services would be quite properly using information in a variety of ways. In the present climate of performance measures, the balance is tipped towards the summative and controlling use of measurement. Those organizations developing a policy for quality would (and should), however, be putting far more emphasis on the developmental use of measurements and indicators as part of an ongoing programme of evaluation and development.

Data collection

How much?

The search for an utterly comprehensive system could lead to mountains of data, taking hours to collect and impossible to analyse or assess. Alternatively, the search for simplicity and manageability could lead to overdependence on one or two methods of collection, and very narrow coverage, resulting in misleading findings.

This tension is very difficult to resolve. In 1992 the Audit Commission (1993a) organized a process of consultation about its 152 proposed Citizen's Charter indicators, which were specifically designed to be of interest to citizens. It received 500 responses, 300 from local authorities, indicating a huge amount of interest. Apart from a widespread concern that national indicators would skew local policies and restrict local choice, a major area of comment concerned the number of indicators. On the one hand, the indicators being suggested were thought to be too many either for 'the citizen' to absorb or to justify the cost of collection; and on the other, it was feared that a mere five or so indicators per service could not adequately reflect complex services, and that those actually proposed paid too little attention to effectiveness, quality or efficiency.

A local approach: self-evaluation

One approach to this problem could be to focus on very local and service-based measurements. At this level, both staff and the public are interested in quite a lot of detail – enough not simply to be able to make some crude comparisons across authorities, but to provide the kind of information discussed in the previous section, that could be used for learning and development.

This approach to quality measurement would put considerable emphasis on self-evaluation, on the responsibility of staff to measure their own work and to have the opportunity to reflect and learn from this. This is not easy, requiring attitudes and cultures that encourage involvement of all staff, that legitimates and makes best use of the time spent on evaluation, and that enables management committees and funders (especially but not exclusively in the voluntary sector) to appreciate the benefits of investing in evaluation as an activity in itself. A project to encourage small voluntary organizations to evaluate their work found that the availability of suitable tools, and help from an interested outsider can be crucial, both in getting self-evaluation started and in helping to sustain it (Thamesdown Evaluation Project 1993).

Quantitative methods: statistical process control

In manufacturing, a key tool in developing quality, strongly emphasized by Deming (for Japanese industry) and by Oakland (for British industry) is the technique known as statistical process control. Oakland suggests that the technique can also be used in non-manufacturing activities. Its aim is to reinforce the philosophy of no-failure, error-free work (Oakland 1989: 180), and to reduce variability, which is seen as the cause of most quality problems.

Earlier discussion about quality systems and the use of standards has raised the question of the relevance of this philosophy to the delivery of high quality public services. If the elimination of variance is given an over-riding priority, this could lead to bureaucratization and standardization of exactly the kind that quality programmes are trying to get away from. However, to the extent that many services, or parts of services, are fairly routine and do require a system of procedures and control to ensure consistency and fairness, the lessons of statistical process (or quality) control (SPC) could be useful. They are described in some detail in W. Edwards Deming's book *Out of the crisis* (1986), where the large number of transactions, the large amount of paper, the large number of procedures but the uncertainty about the 'product', are seen as key differences between service and manufacturing organizations.

The idea of statistical process control is to identify and then measure all the inputs and outputs required for each stage in the achievement of a specified process. Each process then has to be documented (as in a quality assurance system) and monitored to ensure reliability and consistency. This will result in diagrams, charts and graphs which, while not an end in themselves are, Oakland emphasizes, a symbol of the new way of thinking. This, in his view, underlies and forms a vital part of the total quality management approach. Seven methods are suggested: flow charts, check sheets, histograms, Pareto analysis, cause and effect analysis, scatter diagrams and control charts. These can be used to monitor different aspects of the work, such as how it is done, how often, what are the main problems, and what are the differences and variations that need management action.

These techniques are not to be scorned by public service managers, as long as it is remembered what they are being used for and what are their limitations. For example, what are the levels of tolerance between the standard specification and what is acceptable? This is an important question for services where sensitivity to difference, and the use of discretion are accepted as both normal and desirable. Second, might such measurements overwhelm the system, or can they be kept in proportion as one among a set of measurement tools? Third, can staff, consumers and citizens play a part in what appears to be a highly technical and specialized activity?

Management information systems

Statistical process control is one kind of management information system. Other management information systems – the systematic collection of quantitative data by and for managers – are, as already noted (see Burningham 1992) an important feature of performance measurement. I have suggested that some of these, if they help to measure the quality of inputs, throughputs and outputs, can be integrated into the measurement and evaluation of quality. However, many of these systems are of limited value in this respect, being partial, narrow and possibly distorting in their effect on day to day behaviour.

Another source of information held within an organization are client records, or files. An examination of files, for example for medical audit purposes, can reveal deficiencies in record-keeping (Philips 1991), which itself can help improve the future systematic recording of qualitative information and work done. It can also be used as a way of finding out if systems are being operated as intended, as well as a source of information about the treatment of particular conditions.

My own work on quality started with a small-scale examination of files in Birmingham neighbourhood offices, trying to identify by a process of induction the 'quality' elements of the work of staff. This was in an organization that, at that time, had not begun to define quality and where the role of the offices was itself ambiguous and unsupported. The work raised more questions than it answered, but it did show that with relatively little effort and a willingness and interest among staff to allow access to existing sources of information, some qualitatively rich information can be analysed without a great deal of extra data collection effort.

Opinion surveys and market research

Opinion surveys can be as statistically reliable as the measurement of, say, how much traffic passes a given point on a particular day, or how many cases are handled by a social worker in a month. They can provide some fairly basic information about the 'satisfaction' levels and areas of concern as seen by current users of services or by residents in general (National Consumer Council 1991). For organizations that have not moved beyond internal measurement systems, such surveys, whether of staff or public opinion, can be very revealing to managers, councillors and Boards: other points of view exist, and not everyone is necessarily happy with what is on offer!

However, although the practice of finding out the views of the public has been a remarkably recent phenomenon among public service providers (and the practice of finding out staff views seems to be even less well-established), the utility of such surveys can be rather limited. Simple questions of satisfaction are, as I have tried to show in Chapter 3, inadequate without an understanding of peoples' initial expectations and experience. Often, too, the information obtained through opinion research is at too general a level to be used as development tools by front-line managers.

However, it is possible to take a more sophisticated approach to opinion research, in three ways. First, the SERVQUAL instrument shows how the details of quality definitions can provide the basis for appropriate questions.

Second, questionnaires and surveys can be applied to specific groups of users, which leaves room for detailed responses about particular services or the needs of particular groups in the population. They can, in other words, be targeted. Clwyd County Council, for example, rather than having a Council-wide survey, as they and others have so often done, asked departments to bid for the right to have a survey done for their service. Some departments did not bid at all, while others put in a good case (including how the information would be used), which gave them access to the funds allocated for market research (Gaster and Taylor 1993). Simon Speller, testing the Parasuraman gaps model in Stevenage Council, found that those managers who had taken responsibility for their own surveys appeared to have better knowledge and probably a higher commitment to acting on the results than those who were (or were not, as it turned out) receiving the results of MORI surveys commissioned by senior managers.

Third, local people can be involved, both in devising the questionnaires and in carrying out the surveys. This was done for example for day care facilities for the mentally ill in Liverpool in 1991 (Gaster and Rivers 1991). Tenants on housing estates have the capacity and willingness to carry out their own surveys, often with good results, especially if they are supported by community development workers (Smith 1992; Spray 1992).

Finding out users' views

It is not always easy to find out the views of users, yet this is an essential part of quality measurement. Questionnaire surveys are one method, but personal interviews and various forms of dialogue may provide far more telling information.

The National Consumer Council tested this proposition in a guideline study of people with dementia living at home (National Consumer Council 1990). After discussing the issues with carers, experienced researchers interviewed fifteen people in two health authorities (in London and Dorset). Real problems arose because of the varying levels of lucidity, forgetfulness and ability to concentrate, but the conclusion was clear: through deeper insight into the effects of dementia on both sufferers and carers, recommendations could be made to the local health authorities about the need for joint service planning. The interviewers were able to adjust their interviewing techniques to take account of the forgetfulness etc., and to meet the need for constant reassurance. They were thus able to achieve productive interviews.

The use of the word 'reassurance' is significant. It is important for consumers, especially if interviewed while they are still receiving the service in question (as those with a long-term relationship with services must be), to be sure that the information will not be used to their disadvantage, and at the same time to have confidence that it is worth taking the trouble to respond to requests for feedback and information. Sometimes such confidence can be generated by the use of focus groups, where small groups of people in similar circumstances may be asked about their views of the service. Confidentiality can probably more easily be guaranteed if the groups are facilitated by outsiders, but the most important requirement is the ability to run group discussions and to ensure that everyone has their say.

In Delft, an experiment has been in existence since 1988: this is the Citypanel (Severijnen 1994). One thousand people and households are regularly asked their views about different aspects of the City's services, including, specifically, quality (in the form of satisfaction) and work arising from agreed performance targets. A considerable amount of work had to be done to make this process credible to the councillors (after all, it was expensive – and there was also the view that, as elected members, they already knew what local people thought) and to local people (by publishing and publicizing the results and valuing the replies).

Staff, too, had to be convinced, partly of the methodology (this was discussed with the researchers in meetings and workshops), partly of the utility. In practice, over five years, they became involved in deciding the research questions and, with the help of a small financial reward (to be used for self-evaluation) work units and teams were encouraged to use the results. At the same time, the panel has developed into a consultative structure, for particular policies to be debated with target groups and with councillors and staff. This has echoes in the work carried out through neighbourhood forums, user groups and the like throughout the UK, though there are no examples of quite such a comprehensive, continuous and explicit approach to citizen involvement in this country.

Monitoring the service process

While most of the methods mentioned above concentrate on complete episodes (which may themselves be inputs, throughputs or outputs), the importance of the service process as part of quality must not be overlooked. What is the quality of the treatment, the personal interaction between service provider and consumer?

Several ways of monitoring this can be tried, like the mystery customer survey used by Swansea City Council (Opinion Research Services 1993), and the entrance and exit polls developed in Holland as part of their Public Services Quality Monitoring Programme (Schouten and Spapens 1993). In the Dutch example, prior expectations are tested, to be compared with what actually happened at a later date. This information may also be linked to a logbook system, which follows cases down the service chain until the intended service is (or is not?) provided. However, such an approach would have to be done on a selective basis, being very intensive in person-hours, even if a standard system such as that proposed in the Dutch model is used.

It is also more difficult than might be thought to elicit expectations (or possibly hopes) of what the service will be like – as I found when trying a small pilot of my own in Harlow (Gaster 1993a). My research in Birmingham neighbourhood offices showed that 'satisfaction' cards and leaflets to be completed by users also have their limitations. Neighbourhood office staff were helping users to fill in the leaflets (a natural extension of their job, helping with form-filling?) – a process likely to inhibit critical comments – while repairs satisfaction cards were often not returned, in case something went wrong later (Gaster 1991b).

The quality of the exchange between service provider and consumer can be monitored through observation or, if agreement has been negotiated, through video and audio recording (Borzeix 1990). As with all other aspects of quality monitoring, the characteristics of the interpersonal quality being assessed would need to be very clear in order to make sense of the findings.

Research on the quality of housing management and in residential care has shown what is important to service users (and how this compares with what they actually experience): this provides a useful basis for the compilation of checklists (Social Services Inspectorate 1990; Spencer and Walsh 1990). Understanding, listening and knowledgeable staff, privacy and continuity are, for example, highly important to most people, yet these are what many public services are least good at providing.

Complaints

Complaints are an important source of information about what people think of services. By definition, they are always in the form of negative feedback and they are individualistic. They also depend heavily on whether there is a climate where complaints are listened to and acted upon, and whether there is a system that is easy to use and positively encouraged. Research carried out in the 1980s (Seneviratne and Cracknell 1988) showed that, as far as local authorities were concerned, this was rarely the case at that time.

There may, too, be difficulty in deciding what is a complaint. If staff (or a whole organization) are in defensive mode, then any request for action is labelled a complaint, and those who make such requests are trouble-makers. It is only more recently that more positive attitudes have begun to develop, and the rights of citizens to a decent service acknowledged (Atkins 1992). In its training pack for staff, Wolverhampton City Council defined a complaint (covering direct and contracted services but excluding schools and colleges) as:

> Any expression of dissatisfaction about the Council's service provision, e.g. poor service; lack of service; slow service; lack of information; professional decisions; Council policies.
>
>   (Wolverhampton City Council, 1992: overhead 5)

Although much is made of the importance of complaints as a measure of quality in the Citizen's Charter, the Audit Commission, devising the first set of indicators, was cautious about their use (1992: 6). Complaints can indicate both good quality and bad quality: indeed, high numbers may reflect higher quality. One of the aims of a quality policy could well be, in the first instance, to generate public confidence to complain. So complaints statistics, taken on their own, could be very misleading, and comparability pretty well impossible, even between departments of the same organization.

Observation, inspection and audit

The use of checklists to observe, audit or inspect services seems to be increasingly common. In some ways, it has always happened. Schools inspections were audits, and several national organizations (the Health Advisory Service, the Social Services Inspectorate, the Central Council for Education and Training in Social Work, the Economic and Social Research Council and the

University (now Higher Education) Funding Council) have all at various times held inspection visits and audits, carried out by panels of officers, 'experts', peers and lay members. So the notion of audit is not new, though it has, in the new regulatory state referred to earlier (Henkel 1991) become increasingly prominent as a method of monitoring and evaluation.

There are two main disadvantages to this approach, neither of them inevitable. First, such audits seem to be particularly the province of external bodies (or, in the community care field, of arms-length inspection units). They therefore have all the disadvantages noted earlier – of lack of integration with a local policy for quality; lack of ownership and possibly relevance to key players, notably staff; and the consequent probability that the findings will not carry great weight (that is, as far as improving quality is concerned. They may well be – and are – very powerful in the context of resource allocation, contract renewal and so on. But that is not the same thing.)

The second main disadvantage is that the public, as direct or indirect consumers, rarely seem to be involved, except perhaps tokenistically as part of the 'show' on the day of inspection.

However, the publication of tested checklists to reflect core values expected in residential care, for example, can help local authorities develop their own versions and carry out their own audits. Similarly, local authorities wishing to examine their reception services are likely to want to include visual observation, which can be based on checklists developed by others (a 'benchmarking' approach), as well as a variety of other techniques such as consumer surveys and statistical recording of events (unpublished reports from Islington and Hackney Councils).

An issue for any such internal audit is who will carry it out? In 1989, Birmingham Social Services tested a Care Audit system for old people's residential homes using fieldwork staff (Dolan 1989). This seemed quite successful: time was not wasted on familiarization. Even so, each audit took 20 to 40 hours of officer time over two to four weeks, with obvious implications for workloads back at base and overall cost. However, it is clearly important to ensure some distance between the service providers being reviewed and the reviewers, in order to maintain some objectivity. Peer review can otherwise become a secretive and defensive affair, for example, in clinical audit (Pollitt 1987).

Research

A wide range of approaches to measuring, assessing and monitoring service quality exists. Those described above do not even form a comprehensive listing of what is in practice possible. But they give an indication. Some methods will (ought to be?) part of everyday management practice. Some are part of the process of regulation and the attempt to develop national standards. Some are, perhaps, by-products of measurements carried out for other purposes.

As a researcher, it is perhaps appropriate to end this part of the chapter by referring to the role of research. As with most of the other techniques, this can be carried out internally or externally, with and without the help and involvement of the public. Research (and intelligence) can be qualitative or quantitative, regular or one-off, and can focus on the needs and views not only of the public but also of staff and other key stakeholders and interests. It can, as Blackman (1992) argues, provide a different perspective on services from that normally provided by professionals, an adjunct to democracy, and is a vital part of the systematic review of needs and services that ought to inform policy making for the provision and improvement of any public service.

When should measurement take place?

The timing of measurement and monitoring is another chicken and egg question and falls into several parts. The four basic issues are:

1 When to decide on and design a measurement/monitoring system.
2 When to put it into action, and for how long.
3 When to analyse and report on the findings.
4 When to make use of the findings.

Starting points: 'before' and 'after'

It was always a disappointment to me, as a neighbourhood officer in Islington in the first stage of the decentralization programme (1985), that almost no data existed about the pre-existing services, making it impossible to assess what, if any improvements were being bought about by the massive structural and cultural changes involved. This lack of 'before' data was confirmed in a subsequent evaluation of the decentralization policy by Paul Hoggett and Robin Hambleton (Burns et al. 1994), where they take particular note of the late development of management information systems in Islington.

The word 'benchmarking' has been used in two different ways in this book. One is the new, management system sense being promoted in the Welsh Health Service (Bullivant and Naylor 1992), where good practice in other organizations can be used as a learning point for specific procedures and practices in one's own. The other is the more everyday sense, of creating a benchmark (like those up and down the country established years ago by the Ordnance Survey) from which it is possible to take one's bearings and to measure upward or downward progress.

Ideally, any organizational change needs this kind of benchmark, otherwise how can the effect of the change be assessed (assuming the effect of other variables can be identified)? It is particularly necessary for programmes to improve the quality of services.

So an early assessment or audit, using a mixture of measurement methods and certainly including the perceptions of staff and the public, gives a starting point. It provides a baseline for future assessments, and enables a diagnostic evaluation of current services, on which the next stage of the programme would need to be built and with which future change can be compared. The problem often is that the energy needed to bring about the change itself leaves little room for monitoring and measurement: they are put off, or given low priority (the same thing).

Even where the need for baseline measurements is recognised, they are not necessarily to hand and it takes time to develop them. Those Training and Enterprise Councils that were really committed to improving training for people from ethnic minorities found they had to set up data systems from scratch: they did not know enough about when trainees drop out of the system, or who was not getting into it in the first place (Employment Department 1994). It took at least a couple of years to set up a system that would measure what they needed to know.

While some measures need to stay the same so as to enable comparisons over time, some will change or be added, as the nature of the organization and its services change. Measurement does not need to be right first time. An innovative and risk-taking approach is essential, especially in relation to the use of qualitative methods.

Ongoing monitoring and development

After the initial diagnosis, regular checks and measurements will be needed, to provide feedback, food for thought, and to ensure that the programme is continuing on course. Continuing to use a diagnostic and developmental approach, problems can be identified and new ideas tried out.

The exact timing and frequency of such monitoring will vary. In the early stages, it may be more or less continuous, with an inbuilt element of evaluation and discussion. The service design will probably need to be refined, as links in the service chain are more clearly identified and new relationships and cultures begin to emerge. The very process of measurement, the need to be more conscious and explicit about what each person and team within the chain is or should be doing, the narrowing down of key indicators (everyone starts with too many) and the search for appropriate measurement tools are all part of the quality process.

It is at this stage that ownership needs to be developed. Kirklees Council publishes its annual targets and then encourages suggestions for improvement and measurement not just from management and systems analysts but from front-line staff and the public. This policy is beginning to bear fruit, with operational staff making their suggestions straight to the Chief Executive. A new culture is emerging there.

Later on, a more settled pattern may be established, perhaps linking with policy planning and budget cycles. However, if this is done, it needs to be done in a quality way. Some financial or legislative imperatives will always be dictated from outside the organization or work unit. Nevertheless, finance officers and the like need to respond to and support (rather than dictate to) service units. Those responsible for finance and budget preparation ought to be able to produce a timetable of data collection, evaluation and consequent planning that takes into account the needs of the internal 'customer', rather than the other way round.

The final judgment?

If measurement and the results of monitoring are generally used developmentally and diagnostically, on a fairly continuing basis, there comes a time when the needs of public accountability and resource decisions require a more summative approach to data collection. At the personal level, annual performance appraisal systems ensure that individual targets and achievements are regularly assessed. Sometimes, as in the Civil Service, they are overtly used as the basis of promotion decisions, and will include statements of assessment from line managers and possibly others. Sometimes, as with university lecturers, the system is theoretically more developmental, relying on self-evaluation and being used as the basis for planning for the next year.

The same approach can be used organizationally to assess performance compared with intentions. Many local authorities have established performance review committees, where reports on different services are received and recommendations for future action are made. Some, like Lewisham and Kirklees, have developed scrutiny committees, where councillors take an active role in assessing services – their own or those of other authorities providing services to the public, like water. The relationship of these committees with policy, service or area committees may be ambiguous. Nevertheless they do produce some kind of summative statement, enabling service providers and members of the public to stand back from the day to day and to reflect on the impact and outcomes of quality policies.

Quality policies take a long time to put into effect, especially those (and that is probably nearly all of them) that require a complete overhaul of the organizational culture. There would therefore be a lot of sense in trying to identify different phases, and to think what might be achieved within each one. Short-, medium- and long-term targets, suggested in Chapter 6 as an intermediary stage between the minimum and ideal standards, can be developed. If this is done, especially for pilot programmes where politicians and the like are impatient for results, it becomes easier to formulate realistic expectations. This prevents programmes from being written off too soon, at too early a point on the learning curve (Gaster and Taylor 1993: 17).

Using the results

Finally, it is worth noting that monitoring and evaluation do not necessarily generate immediate results. First, they have to reach key people. Then they need to be considered carefully, perhaps in the light of new circumstances, perhaps allowing time for reflection and consultation on the accuracy and relevance of the findings themselves.

Only after the results begin to be owned will they be used as a practical part of the quality cycle. Sometimes, for those who have put a lot of effort into designing and collecting data, the time lapse can be disappointingly long. However, if the process is fully integrated with the quality policy, the results should eventually come into their own. It can take months, sometimes years.

Criteria for evaluation

In measuring something called 'quality', there are two distinct elements. First, there is the nature and level of the service quality itself, defined in the variety of ways discussed earlier in the book, and relating to targets and standards that may be developed internally and, sometimes, externally. Second, there is the relationship between quality systems and the actual quality being produced. If the outright measurement of quality is difficult – and everyone says it is – then how much more difficult it is to assess the effects of activities to develop and promote that quality. Yet this is an important issue, especially for managers who may fear that their energies are being diverted into the developing and managing fashionable processes whose effectiveness cannot be proved.

Indicators and measures of service quality, of the conformance to specification, of fitness for purpose, of interpersonal and process quality, and of the quality of the environment are beginning to emerge. They can also be developed to measure inputs, throughputs and outputs, possibly also for outcomes. The criteria for an evaluation then depends on the level it is thought these indicators should reach at specified moments in the life cycle of service improvement. Is the quality high, low or somewhere in between, and is it improving? Is action needed in order to make progress?

Deciding criteria for evaluating the suitability and relevance of a particular quality programme is another matter. Reports on how and whether quality assurance schemes, total quality management programmes, quality circles and other formulations actually affect quality improvements are uncommon. The gurus who promote such schemes do not, on the whole, come up with evidence about their effectiveness. When so many other factors, including economic recession, affect the survival and profit rates of private companies, it would require a very wide-ranging comparative study to see if those firms with well-established quality systems are the ones that have survived. Counting the number of staff suggestions for improvement might indicate the arrival of a new quality culture, but establishing a causal link between quality programmes and economic survival could be very difficult, especially when such programmes (in the UK at least) have only caught on in the last five years or so.

Causal connections between programmes and results are even more difficult to identify in public services, where there is no profit measure, and where many other factors, especially political and ideological ones, affect the chances of survival. It is, however, vital to think about these matters. Far too many new public management practices are being transferred into a public service context without sufficient thought about their appropriateness or chances of success. Research is needed over the next few years to begin to rectify this omission. This could help to make explicit the role of quality programmes in improving the quality of services experienced by the public.

8

Choices for quality

The future of quality in the public services

Although anyone with a commitment to public service and to the provision of 'public services' would want them to be of as good quality as possible, there are many who might very reasonably be sceptical about the need for new policies and practices going under the separate label of 'quality'. There have already been a lot of management fads in the 1970s and 1980s, all designed to improve services: is quality one of these, or is it something that will or should be more enduring?

The aim of this final chapter is to bring together, as succinctly as possible, the main themes and dilemmas arising from the aspects of quality considered in the rest of the book. Looking to the future, managers of public services – services to the public – need both practical tools and frameworks for thinking and keeping hold of ideals in the face of endless pressure and the spectre of despair. Is the improvement of quality an entirely incremental, pragmatic process, or can some theory be brought into play to make sense of how quality might be perceived in public services? If the notion of quality is democratic and participative, aiming to increase sensitivity while retaining fairness and consistency, are there forces, pressures and constraints that militate against successful implementation? Is high quality too expensive? Is it too difficult?

What kind of quality?

The intention of this book has been to make the case for treating the need to improve quality in public services as a serious issue, warranting careful, systematic and thoughtful attention.

I have tried to show that the apparently simple language of quality needs to be unravelled, and that recipes cooked up by quality gurus are not necessarily applicable to services governed by other motives than increasing profits and market share. Nevertheless, there are useful lessons to be learnt from the private sector – where the 'quality thing' started – not least the need for attention to detail and a systematic approach if public services are to be more consistent and of a higher standard than in the past.

Based on a rational model of policy implementation (whose strengths and weaknesses are analysed in Chapter 1) the essence of public service quality is, I think, as follows:

1 It is value-based. Unless those defining and putting into practice activities to improve the quality of their services are clear about the underlying values that should be driving the organization and all those working for it, 'quality' becomes a empty slogan. In that case, it is unlikely to meet the needs of those whom it is intended to benefit. If values are clear and explicit, then strategic and operational objectives can be formulated as the basis for deciding the service specification. How quality is viewed will be very different if the prime values are equity, efficiency, equality, democracy and partnership, than if they are competition, non-intervention, economy, consumerism.

2 Quality is not a purely managerial concern. It needs the input, support and commitment of politicians. It also requires a sense of ownership and involvement from staff, consumers and members of the public, arising from real (not token) consultation and participation.

3 Relationships with customers need special consideration. Public services are different from private ones and also, in a rather different way, from those provided by the voluntary sector (though the contract culture, where private and voluntary organizations are responsible for the day-to-day delivery of public services, is blurring the boundaries here). Universal, preventative, rationed or compulsory services produce entirely different relationships with consumers (not customers) from those where choice is available (although choice is, of course, often restricted in the private sector through monopolistic and restrictive practices). The needs of those excluded from access to services for a whole series of reasons (discrimination among them) have to be taken into account. The impact of public services on society at large – the externalities or spillover effects – have to be taken into consideration in a way that is not on the whole required of the private sector. The public has rights over public services and it has duties towards them that are not replicated in the private sector: citizens need to know and have a say about services and their quality.

4 Defining quality is not easy, and the existence of different, competing priorities makes it even more complicated. Nevertheless, a framework of

dimensions (technical, non-technical and environmental), an understanding of inputs, throughputs and outputs, and an analysis of the differences between expectations, experience and satisfaction can all contribute to a definition of the quality characteristics of specific services. A process of negotiation, informed by the values and objectives referred to in (1) above, will produce trade-offs. Some quality characteristics will be given higher priority than others. The level of quality achievable over a defined period, within existing resources and other constraints affecting public services, can then be clarified and agreed. It may be as important to say what is not included as to state what is.

5 So quality standards (that is, defined levels of quality) are not objective, scientific facts. They are the result of an untidy process of negotiation between key interests. Ideal (not perfect) standards, and achievable and minimum standards can be differentiated. It needs to be clear, at different stages in the quality cycle, which of these is the basis of measurement and evaluation.

6 Putting a quality policy into practice is even more difficult than defining it. This is the territory of the gurus, where particular wariness is needed to make sure that solutions derived from a manufacturing, profit driven context are in fact applicable to public services. Most existing systems (quality assurance and control, total quality management, customer care, quality standards and contracts) are, on closer examination defined differently and are defective in a variety of ways. They generally cover only part of the requirements for a comprehensive quality system. Quality systems for public services need to take into account the following:

- Public sector values.
- Democratic, professional and managerial lines of accountability.
- The full range of relationships with the public, as consumers and citizens.
- Long and complex service chains.
- Legal, financial, policy and political frameworks for action.

7 Measuring quality is a must in a serious programme to improve public services. Imaginative qualitative as well as quantitative methods can provide the basis for evaluating current standards and future progress, and for deciding future action. Measurement and monitoring to improve quality ought to emphasize the developmental, diagnostic, formative type of measure and methods of feedback, but summative assessments, relating to defined targets, are probably also essential. What is unhelpful and possibly undermining is the exclusive use of quantitative, externally determined indicators and measurements that are used judgmentally, as a form of control. If such measurements are used, as part of resource allocation or for other managerial or political reasons, they should not be confused with quality measurements.

8 Regular built-in review, evaluation and planning processes, involving representatives of key interests, can help redefine quality. They can refocus the quality policy and programme in the light of changing needs and priorities.

9 One thing is certain. A quality programme takes a long time, three to five years at the minimum. During this time, the ideal would be for a quality

culture to emerge. This is a culture where it is normal to be clear what is to be done, to try to do it, to be willing to account for it, and to work closely with others to achieve it. Unfortunately, this kind of culture is not the norm in public services. Where there are current efforts to make it so, as in some of the approaches to the new public management, countervailing forces are at work. Organizations providing or responsible for public services are being forced to introduce systems and procedures that could result in lower, not higher quality. It is on some of these tensions that the rest of the chapter concentrates.

Tensions and contradictions

Quality in public services is, then, by no means a simple matter. Managers convinced that it is necessary to check and improve the quality of their services, whether as a direct provider or as the 'purchaser' or 'client' of other organizations, have to make choices all along the way. However, that choice is not necessarily free. Controls and constraints come from all angles, and it would be the rare manager who had a free hand. Managers should be able to deal with complexities and constraints, and should not be seeking simple (simplistic?) solutions to complicated problems.

Some tensions and pressures are stronger than others, especially those coming from the outside world and from Central Government. Most of them are illustrated in the following pairings:

- Political/managerial.
- Managerial/professional.
- Standards/standardization.
- Competition/collaboration.
- Short term/long term.

Political versus managerial and managerial versus professional quality

'Quality', through the emphasis on the Citizen's Charter, the promotion of national standards and performance indicators, the development of the national curriculum and other centralising tendencies, is becoming the province of political ideology. The danger is that in the process the very concept will become devalued. So managers responsible for public services need to be able to retain ownership of ideas about and processes for improvement. If necessary, they must resist pressures (where they can) which, under the same name of 'quality', diminish local freedoms to negotiate standards, to develop processes and to provide developmental feedback that will enable services to meet local or very specific and different needs.

To do this, and to ensure that the local version of quality is accountable and politically legitimated, it is crucial to understand the political nature of quality. It is not simply a managerial process, but part of the way that publicly funded bodies account for their activities. The policy and accountability aspects of quality therefore have to be developed by and with politicians and local people who represent the public interest and are (sometimes) elected by the public for that purpose.

It is unfortunate that quality has so far been interpreted very much as the province of 'the manager'. It is certainly time to follow the lead of some of the pioneering local authorities, where a new relationship between Council and residents was signalled by their (earlier) versions of Citizens' Charters

At the same time, managers have to steer a course which, while acknowledging the claims of professionals to a professional ethos that automatically ensures high quality services, also balances other considerations, such as the consumer and citizen perspective and the need for more explicit and better publicized forms of accountability.

These processes of holding the ring, of developing and maintaining processes of negotiation between different interests, often with different levels of power, while at the same time ensuring a trusting and credible relationship with different groups in the community, are not easy. Managers used to hierarchical and departmental modes of service production, where possibly the main debate about service improvement, if any, has been in the context of industrial relations, may feel more comfortable with a directive, top-down style of management based on the assumption of conflict.

Nowadays, a more enabling approach is required, where different opinions can be safely aired and properly listened to, and where a process of constructive negotiation takes place. Networking and listening (not purely female qualities, I hope, though this is often said) are the keys to this type of management. It is different from the traditional style and may be at odds not only with the past, but with the other demands that modern public service managers have to meet.

Standards versus standardization

One of the most difficult balances that managers will have to weigh up is between making services more consistent and reliable, and making them more flexible and responsive. Both are needed for high quality services. However, as the recent debate on the national curriculum has demonstrated, too much insistence on central standards leads to amazing amounts of bureaucracy, a drastic reduction in the local use of discretion, the failure to meet different consumer needs or to encourage innovation and experiment, low morale among service producers (teachers) and the actual reduction of educational quality for pupils (and therefore for parents, the community and the country).

This is perhaps an extreme (though real) example of standardizing tendencies. If they are complemented by approaches to implementing quality drawn from the manufacturing sector, where the emphasis (in total quality management, quality control and quality assurance schemes) is indeed on standardization and on the reduction of error, the combination could be lethal.

Added to this is the standardizing and fossilizing tendency induced by contract specification. The notion of flexible, integrated services may be difficult to sustain. It is proving difficult (but not impossible) to involve the public in the process of contract specification. This may be for technical reasons, for often spurious commercial confidentiality reasons, or because the main actors, the providers and purchasers, are too preoccupied with maintaining their own positions to allow others into the debate. How, then, can purchasers and providers know whether they are providing the kind of quality most relevant to the differing needs and requirements of the public?

While considerations of equity and equality must not be lost, the fight on the hands of public service managers may well be that of retaining the right to make decisions most suited to the actual circumstances, rather than providing standard replies to non-standard problems. Procrustus, the inn-keeper in the Greek myth, had beds to fit every guest. If visitors were too short, they were stretched on a rack; if too long, their legs were amputated. Will consumers still have to fit the service in the future, or can we at last move to a point where the service fits the consumer?

Competition versus collaboration

An important concept for quality is that of the service chain. This, as explained in Chapter 4, is the series of links between different actions that together make up the complete service. In a high quality service, there will be no weak links, and the connections between each one will be firm, explicit and well co-ordinated. The implication is that activities that increase co-operation and collaboration, that are bound together by similar sets of values and are aimed towards achieving the same objectives, will be activities that help improve service quality. Conversely, divisive tendencies, which emphasize the role of the individual rather than the team, which accentuate the different roles of departments and organizations, which encourage a 'pass the buck' and 'it's not my responsibility' mentality are inimical to quality improvements.

There is, therefore, a real tension between the forces that encourage divisiveness and competition – contracts and privatization, league tables and performance-related pay – but which at the same time *may* have the effect of increasing choice (for institutional purchasers, not necessarily for consumers) and those forces, deriving from collectivist ideologies, that encourage working together and mutual support.

It is not logically necessary to make a strict division between the two sets of forces. However, in practice they appear to be mutually exclusive. Those public sector managers who favour a more collaborative and enabling approach are very often those who are eased out of their posts (for example when the Chief Executives of Health Trusts are appointed) by the forces favouring a more 'macho' approach to management. This does not augur well for the kind of quality discussed in this book. It is also, interestingly enough, exactly the opposite of the kind of manager required by even the most standardizing of the gurus. They all recommend management styles that drive out fear, that encourage worker participation, that reward team work. It is quite a paradox!

Short term versus long term

There are plenty of other sources of anxiety and pressure facing managers interested in improving quality. However, the question of short-termism, and the effect this has on thinking about quality and in particular the costs of quality is the last I shall consider here.

In some of its earliest work, the Audit Commission (1984, 1985) noted the perverse effects of one-year budget cycles on the efficient and effective use of capital resources and on policy planning. In public services, such time horizons are still the norm. This makes it difficult, though not impossible, to develop longer-term programmes for improvement. Luckily, the current fashion for strategic planning is an example of longer-term thinking that could be a positive aid in the development of quality programmes.

However, there is always the danger that new requirements and imperatives will sweep away the long term in favour of the short term. This danger is even more real for programmes where there is a high initial financial cost and where the benefits are more difficult both to quantify and to predict. Organizations tempted to play safe – encouraged by the current political climate in which public services have to operate – could easily abandon policies and programmes to improve quality which, with their long time scales, do not fit into immediate priorities. One of the lessons from Japanese industry is the twenty-year timescales on which investment is often planned. It is not suggested that the return on quality investment would take that long (this would imply starting with children in their cradles). Behaviour and attitudes do, given encouragement, change over shorter periods. But given the need to raise awareness and begin to define quality, develop (or make explicit) values and objectives, identify stakeholders and interests and get them involved, carry out an organizational diagnosis, develop action plans and service standards, provide training and support and make structural changes where necessary, there is no way that a policy for quality can be seen as a 'quick fix'.

The psychology of quality improvement is, therefore, that it is an investment, which could and should produce substantial returns. These include: clarity about the purpose and nature of services, better designed services, fewer mistakes, less time spent on redressing grievances, higher levels of satisfaction, better targeted resources, clearer and more effective accountability, a better relationship with the public, a better trained workforce and a more involved public.

On the other hand, the costs of devoting resources to policy development and implementation, to training, consultation and measurement, to managing change and developing a new culture, are likely to be more obvious and more imperative. Developing realistic expectations of what can be achieved when – and monitoring and feeding back information about progress – is probably hard in the face of political and financial pressures. If public services are to survive, this must be done.

A theory of quality?

The management of quality in the public services depends on a number of assumptions about the nature of those services and the relationship between the providers and the public. While these relationships are becoming increasingly complex, and the definition of a 'public service' increasingly hard to pin down, some ideas exist that can help to explain the idea of 'public service quality'. At the same time, it is necessary to reject other ideas that are leading to spurious and misleading interpretations, which simply encourage public and employee cynicism and which may have the effect of actually reducing existing quality.

Taking the last point first, it seems that much of the philosophy driving Charterism and the associated practices of privatization, forced competition, league tables and an emphasis on complaints as the only form of citizen redress is the theory of public choice. This assumes that individuals will always behave rationally in their own interest and that they will have the power to choose and, if they so decide, not to use the service – to exit. Even if this were generally true (which I doubt), I have argued in this book that consumers of public services would not have this power, even if all services were put out to tender or otherwise privatized. Other theories of human behaviour are needed.

I suggest that a pluralistic explanation, which assumes that a range of interests may compete or collaborate in the production and consumption of public services, is more appropriate. This allows for the use of 'voice' as well as of 'exit' or 'choice' as a response to service provision. It explains why a more active role for consumers and citizens is required if services are truly to begin to be of a high quality. It allows for altruistic behaviour and ensures that the role of workers at all levels is valued. The notion of pluralism is also helpful in remembering that people have different roles: people are at the same time consumers and citizens, employees and voters, professionals and politicians. Each has a part to play in quality, in the cycle of policy development and implementation that is at the root of the process.

Recognizing and welcoming this diversity and complexity is what quality ought to be about. Public service quality is a collective enterprise: it will not thrive on individualism, divisiveness and standardization. It is an essential part of a modern manager's tools for the job, requiring a combination of open-mindedness, precision and responsiveness and depending, in the end, on old-fashioned but still much-needed public sector values.

Bibliography

Ashrif, Humaira (1993) *Total quality management within high union density organisations.* Dissertation for MSc in Management Development and Social Responsibility, School for Advanced Urban Studies, University of Bristol (unpublished).

Association of Metropolitan Authorities (1991a) *Quality services: an introduction to quality assurance for local authorities.* London: AMA.

Association of Metropolitan Authorities (1991b) *Agreeing on quality?* London: AMA.

Atkins, Robert (1992) 'Making use of complaints: Braintree District Council' *Local Government Studies,* 18(3): 164–71.

Audit Commission (1984) *The impact on local authorities' economy, efficiency and effectiveness of the block grant distribution system.* London: HMSO.

Audit Commission (1985) *Capital expenditure controls in local government in England.* London: HMSO.

Audit Commission (1989) *Managing services effectively: performance review.* Audit Commission Management paper No. 5. London: HMSO.

Audit Commission (1992) *Citizen's Charter indicators: consultation paper.* London: Directorate of Management Practice.

Audit Commission (1993a) *Citizen's Charter indicators: charting a course.* London: HMSO.

Audit Commission (1993b) *Their health, your business: the new role of the District Health Authority.* London: HMSO.

Audit Commission (1993c) *Putting quality on the map: measuring and appraising quality in the public service.* London: HMSO.

Barnes, M. and Wistow, G. (1992) *Researching user involvement.* University of Leeds. Nuffield Institute for Health Service Studies.

Benington, J. and Taylor, M. (1992) 'The renewal of quality in the political process', in I. Sanderson (ed.) *Management of quality in local government.* Warwick Series in Local Economic and Social Strategy. Harlow: Longmans.

Beresford, P. and Croft, S. (1993) *Citizen involvement: a practical guide for change*. London: Macmillan.

Blackman, T. (1992) 'Improving quality through research', in I. Sanderson (ed.) *Management of quality in local government*, Warwick Series in Local Economic and Social Strategy. Harlow: Longmans.

Borzeix, A. (1990) 'Mais qu'est-ce que la qualité d'un service publique?' Paper presented to CNRS conference *A quoi servent les usagers?*, Paris, 1991 (unpublished).

Bowness, B. (1993) *Participation in health care: a realistic objective?* Unpublished dissertation, MSc in Policy Studies, University of Bristol.

Bouckaert, G. (1990) *Productivity measurement: certain diseases and uncertain cures*. Paper to Fourth National Public Sector Productivity Conference, Albany, New York (Catholic University of Leuven, Belgium, unpublished).

Bouckaert, G. and Pollitt, C. (forthcoming) *Quality improvement in European public services*. London: Sage Publications.

Bovaird, A.C. (1975) 'Analytical techniques for performance review', *Corporate Planning*, 2(3): 26–39.

Bramley, G. and Le Grand, J. (1992) *Who uses local services? – Striving for equity*. The Belgrave Papers, No. 4, Luton, Local Government Management Board

Bullivant, J. and Naylor, M. (1992) 'Best of the best', *Health Service Journal*, 27 August 1992, pp. 24–5.

Burningham, D. (1992) *Quality measurement and management in local government*. Paper to the Study Group on quality and productivity in the public services, 1992 Conference of the European Group on Public Administration, Pisa, Italy. Centre for the Evaluation of Public Policy and Practice, Brunel University.

Burns, D., Hambleton, R. and Hoggett, P. (1994) *The politics of decentralisation: revitalising local democracy*. Public Policy and Politics Series, London: Macmillan.

Caplen, R.H. (1982) *A practical approach to quality control*. (4th ed.) London: Hutchinson Business Books.

Carter, N. (1989) 'Performance indicators: "backseat driving" or "hands-off" control?', *Policy and Politics*, 17(2): 131–8.

Carter, N. (1991) 'Learning to measure performance: the use of indicators in organisations', *Public Administration*, 69: 85–101.

Cassam, E. and Gupta, H. (1992) *Quality assurance in social care agencies: a practical guide*. Harlow: Longmans.

Centre for the Evaluation of Public Policy and Practice (1992) *Considering quality: an analytical guide to the literature on quality standards in the public services*. London: Brunel University.

Centre for Health Economics (1991a) *Quality management initiatives in the NHS: Strategic approaches to improving quality*, QMI Series No. 3, University of York.

Centre for Health Economics (1991b) *Quality management initiatives in the NHS: Patient Information Survey*. QMI Series No. 4, University of York.

Clarke, M. and Stewart, J. (1987) 'The public service orientation and the citizen', *Local Government Policy Making*, 14(1): 34–40.

Clifford, C. (1993) *The Citizen's Charter, quality and the Civil Service*. Paper to the Political Studies Association of the U.K., Annual Conference, University of Leicester, 20–22 April.

Confederation of British Industries (1988) *Zero defects – a new British standard?* Royston: Rooster Books Ltd.

Crosby, P. (1986) *Quality without tears: the art of hassle-free management*. New York McGraw-Hill International Edition Management Series.

Czepiel, J.A., Solomon, M.R. and Surprenant, C.F. (Eds) (1985) *The service encounter: managing employee/customer interaction in service businesses*. Lexington, MA: Lexington Books.

Dale, B. (1986) 'Experience with quality circles and quality costs', in B. Moores (ed.) *Are they being served?* Hemel Hempstead: Prentice Hall.

Davis, H. and Stewart, J. (1993) *The growth of government by appointment: implications for local democracy*. Luton: Local Government Management Board.

Day, P. and Klein, R. (1987): *Accountabilities: five public services*. Tavistock Publications.

Day, Tony (1990) *Getting closer to the consumer? Locality planning in Exeter Health District*. School for Advanced Urban Studies Working paper 84.

Deakin, Nicholas (1994) *The politics of welfare* (2nd ed.). Hemel Hempstead: Harvester Wheatsheaf.

Deakin, N. and Wright, A. (eds) (1990) *Consuming public services*. London: Routledge.

Deming, W.E. (1986) *Out of the crisis: quality, productivity and competitive production*. Cambridge, MA: Press Syndicate, University of Cambridge.

Devon County Council (1993) *Quality standards: Directory, Volume One*. Exeter: Social Services Department.

Dolan, P. (1989) *Standards of care audit, pilot exercise, report for feedback*. Birmingham: Social Services Department, Birmingham City Council (unpublished).

Donabedian, A. (1980, 1982, 1985) *Explorations in quality assessment and monitoring: Vol. 1: The definition of quality and approaches to its assessment; Vol 2: The criteria and standards of quality; Vol 3: The methods and findings of quality assessment and monitoring*. Ann Arbor, MI: Health Administration Press.

Dunleavy, P. (1991) *Democracy, bureaucracy and public choice: economic explanations in political science*. Hemel Hempstead: Harvester Wheatsheaf.

Ellis, R. (ed) (1988) *Professional competence and quality assurance in the caring professions*. London: Chapman and Hall.

Employment Department (1994) *TECS and provision for people from ethnic minorities*. London: HMSO.

Everitt, T. (1990) *Users' views of health visiting services: a literature review*. Quality management and research programme. Birmingham: Department of Social policy and Social Work, University of Birmingham.

Foster, J. and Crawley, C. (1993) 'Quality, equality and Europe', *RSA Journal*, April, 282–295.

Freeman-Bell, G. and Grover, R. (1993a) 'Quality management and local authorities', in C. Armistead and A. Payne (eds) *Service Sector Management Research Biennial Symposium* Cranfield: Cranfield School of Management.

Freeman-Bell, G. and Grover, R. (1993b) 'The costs of quality in local government', in R. Johnston and N.D.C. Slack (eds) *Service superiority: the design and delivery of effective service operations*. Warwick Business School, University of Warwick: Operations Management Association, UK.

Freeman-Bell, G. and Grover, R. (forthcoming) 'The use of quality management in local authorities', in *Local Government Studies*.

Gaster, L. (1990) 'Defining and measuring quality: does decentralisation help?' *Local Government Policy Making*, 17(2): 15–23.

Gaster, L. (1991a) 'Quality and decentralisation: are they connected?' *Policy and Politics*, 19(4): 257–267.

Gaster, L. (1991b) *Quality at the front line*. Bristol: Decentralisation Research and Information Centre, School for Advanced Urban Studies, University of Bristol.

Gaster, L. (1992a) 'Quality, devolution and decentralisation', in I. Sanderson (ed)

Management for quality in local government. Warwick Series in Local Economic and Social Strategy. Harlow: Longmans.

Gaster, L. (1992b) *Quality, choice and efficiency: the case of neighbourhood offices.* Paper to the Study Group on Quality and Productivity. Pisa: European Group on Public Administration. (Revised for *Local Government Policy Making* (1994), 20(4): 18–23.)

Gaster, L. (1992c) 'Quality in service delivery: competition for resources or more effective use of resources?' *Local Government Policy Making*, 19(1): 55–64.

Gaster, L. (1993a) *Organisational change and political will: monitoring and evaluating decentralisation and democratisation in Harlow.* Bristol: Decentralisation Research and Information Centre, School for Advanced Urban Studies, University of Bristol.

Gaster, L. (1993b) 'Neighbourhood centres and community care in Liverpool', in R. Smith *et al.* (eds) *Working together for better community care.* SAUS Study. Bristol: School for Advanced Urban Studies, University of Bristol.

Gaster, L. (forthcoming) 'Quality in welfare services', in David Gladstone (ed) *British social welfare past, present and future.* London: UCL Press.

Gaster, L. (forthcoming) 'Quality in service contracts at the local level: the case on environmental services in Harlow District Council', in G. Bouckaert and C. Pollitt (eds) *Quality Improvement in European Public Services.* London: Sage.

Gaster, L. and Hoggett, P. (1993) 'Neighbourhood decentralisation and local management', in N. Thomas, N. Deakin and J. Doling (eds) *Learning from innovation: housing and social care in the 1990s.* Birmingham: Birmingham Academic Press.

Gaster, L. and Rivers, A. (1991) *Liverpool City Council: day to day service delivery in Granby–Toxteth.* Report to the City Council. Bristol: School for Advanced Urban Studies, University of Bristol, (unpublished).

Gaster, L., Martin, L., Doogan, K., Stewart, M. and Hoggett, P. (1992) *Bradford Council's Policy of Community Government.* Report to Bradford City Council. Bristol: School for Advanced Urban Studies (unpublished).

Gaster, L. and Taylor, M. (1993) *Learning from consumers and citizens.* Luton: Local Government Management Board.

Gosschalk, B. (1989) 'In the eyes of the users', *Municipal Review and AMA News*, September, 120–1.

Gyford, J. (1991) *Citizens, consumers and councils: local government and the public.* Government beyond the centre series, ed. Gerry Stoker and Steve Leach, Macmillan Education.

Ham, C. (1992): *Locality purchasing.* Health Services Management Centre, Discussion Paper 30. Birmingham: University of Birmingham.

Hambleton, R. and Hoggett, P. (1990) *Beyond excellence: quality local government in the 1990s.* School for Advanced Urban Studies Working paper 85. Bristol: University of Bristol.

Harlow District Council (1990) *Moving Forward in 1990–91 and beyond.* Harlow: Harlow Council.

Harrison, L. (1993) 'Newcastle's mental health consumer group: a case study of user involvement', in R. Smith *et al.* (eds) *Working together for better community care.* SAUS Study. School for Advanced Urban Studies. Bristol: University of Bristol.

Heald, G. and Stodel, E. (1988) *Supplementary Benefit claimants: expectations and experience of the service provided by DHSS's local offices.* London: HMSO.

Henkel, M. (1991) 'The new "evaluative" state', *Public Administration*, 69 (Spring), 121–36.

HMSO (1991) *The Citizen's Charter: a guide.* (Summary of proposals in Government White Paper of the same name), Cm 1599, July.

HMSO (1991) *The citizen's charter*. Cm 1599, July.

HMSO (1992) *The citizen's charter – first report: 1992*. Cm 2101.

Hoggett, P. (1991) 'A new management in the public sector?' *Policy and Politics*, 19(4): 243–56.

Hoyes, L., Means, R. and Le Grand, J. (1991) *Made to measure? Performance indicators, performance measures and the reform of community care*. Bristol: School for Advanced Urban Studies, University of Bristol.

Humbert, M., Meijer, J., Nieuwenhuis, M. and Schouten, R. (1992) *Government Service Centres: final report*. Study carried out on behalf of the Directorate of Inter-ministerial Affairs and Information, Ministry of Home affairs, Holland. The Hague: B and A Group Policy Research and Advice BV.

Hutchins, D. (1990) *In pursuit of quality: participative techniques for quality improvement*. London: Pitman.

Institute of Local Government Studies (1989) *Improving the quality of local authority housing management*. Birmingham: Joseph Rowntree Foundation and the University of Birmingham.

James, K. (1989) 'Encounter analysis: front-line conversations and their role in improving customer service', *Local Government Studies*, 15(3): 11–24.

Jones, J. (1991) 'Government "is misguided over health strategy" ', *The Independent*, 18 November: 8.

Joss, R., Kogan, M., Henkel, M. and Spink, M. (1991–2) *Evaluation of Total Quality Management Projects in the National Health Service: First and second interim reports*. Uxbridge: Centre for the Evaluation of Public Policy and Practice, Brunel University.

Juran, J.M. (1979) *Quality control handbook* (3rd ed). New York: McGraw-Hill.

Le Grand, J. and Robinson, R. (1984) *The economics of social problems: the market versus the state* (2nd ed.). London: Macmillan Education.

Lipsky, M. (1980) *Street-level bureaucracy: dilemmas of the individual in public services*. New York: Russell Sage Foundation.

Local Government Information Unit (1991) *Quality and equality*. New directions in Local Government 3. London: Local Government Information Unit.

Local Government Management Board (1992) *Quality and equality: service to the whole community*. Luton: Local Government Management Board.

Local Government Management Board (1993a) *Challenge and Change: characteristics of good management in local government*. Luton: Local Government Management Board.

Local Government Management Board (1993b) *Local government community leadership: the strategic role of the local authority*. Luton: Local Government Management Board.

Maister, D.H. (1985) 'The psychology of waiting lines', in J. Czepiel *et al. The service encounter: managing employee/customer interaction in service businesses*. Lexington, MA: Lexington Books.

Martin, L. (1993) *User involvement in community care in Wiltshire*. Bristol: School for Advanced Urban Studies, University of Bristol (unpublished).

Martin, L. and Gaster, L. (1993) 'Community care planning in Wolverhampton: involving the voluntary sector and black and minority ethnic groups', in R. Smith *et al. Working together for better community care*. SAUS Study. School for Advanced Urban Studies. Bristol: University of Bristol.

Miller, C. (1991) *Public service trade unionism and the democratisation of the local state*. PhD thesis, School for Advanced Urban Studies. Bristol: University of Bristol (unpublished).

Morgan, J. and Everitt, T. (1990) 'Introducing quality management in the NHS', *International Journal of Health Care Management*, 3(5): 23–36.

Moores, B. (ed) (1986) *Are they being served?* Hemel Hempstead: Philip Allen.

National Consumer Council (1986) *Measuring up: a consumer assessment of local authority services: a guideline study*. London: National Consumer Council.

National Consumer Council (1990) *Consulting consumers in the NHS: a guideline study – services for elderly people with dementia living at home*. London: National Consumer Council.

National Consumer Council (1991) *Consumer concerns 1991: consumer views of public and local services*. London: National Consumer Council.

Nicholson, N. (1993) *Performance indicators: an introductory guide*. Luton: Policy and Performance Review Network and Local Government Management Board.

Norah Fry Research Centre (1990) *The group in action (group leaders' manual, field-testing pack No 2)*. Quality in action project. Bristol: University of Bristol.

Nove, A. (1993) 'Perverse results of a red tape revolution', *The Guardian*, 15 November.

Nyquist, J.D, Bitner, M.J. and Booms, B.H. (1985) 'Identifying communication difficulties in the service encounter: a critical incident approach', in J. Czepiel *et al* (eds) *The service encounter: Managing employee/customer interaction in service businesses*. Lexington, MA: Lexington Books.

Oakland, J.S. (1989) *Total quality management*. London: Butterworth/Heinemann.

Opinion Research Services (1993) *Mystery customer survey for Swansea City Council*. Swansea: Opinion Research Services, University College of Swansea.

Paddon, M. (1992) 'Quality in an enabling context', in I. Sanderson (ed.) *Management of quality in local government*. Warwick Series in Local Economic and Social Strategy. Harlow: Longmans.

Parasuraman, A., Zeithaml, V.A. and Berry, L.L. (1988a) 'A conceptual model of service quality and its implications for future research', *Journal of Marketing*, 49 (Fall): 41–50.

Parasuraman, A., Zeithaml, V.A. and Berry, L.L. (1988b) 'SERVQUAL: a multiple item scale for measuring consumer perceptions of service quality', *Journal of Retailing*, 64(1): 12–40.

Peters, T.J. and Waterman, R.H. (1982) *In search of excellence: lessons from America's best run companies*. New York: Harper Collins.

Pfeffer, N. and Coote, A. (1991) *Is quality good for you?* Social Policy Paper No 5, London, Institute for Public Policy Research.

Philips, P. (1991) 'Case notes audit', in *Network: a newsletter for medical audit assistants*, The Kings Fund Centre for Health Services Development, Issue 1, April 1991, 7–9.

Pirsig, R.M. (1974) *Zen and the art of motorcycle maintenance: an enquiry into values*. London: Vintage.

Pollitt, C. (1987) 'Capturing quality? The quality issue in British and American health policies', *Journal of Public Policy*, 7(1): 71–92.

Pollitt, C. (1988) 'Bringing consumers into performance measurement: concepts, consequences and constraints', *Policy and Politics*, 16(2): 77–87.

Pollitt, C. (1990) 'Doing business in the temple? Managers and quality assurance in the public services', *Public Administration*, 68(4): 435–52.

Pollitt, C. (1993) *Management and the public services*. (2nd ed.). Oxford: Blackwell Publishers.

Prior, D., Stewart, J. and Walsh, K. (1993) *Is the Citizen's Charter a charter for citizens?* The Belgrave Papers, No. 7. Luton: Local Government Management Board.

Propper, C. (1992) *Quasi-markets, contracts and quality*, Studies in decentralisation and quasi-markets No. 9. Bristol: School for Advanced Urban Studies, University of Bristol.

Sanderson, Ian (ed) (1992) *Management of quality in local government*. Warwick Series in Local Economic and Social Strategy. Harlow: Longmans.

Schon, D.A. (1971) *Beyond the stable state*. Aldershot: Temple Smith.

Schouten, R. and Spapens, T. (1993) *The public services quality monitoring system*. The Hague: the B and A Group to the Ministry of Home Affairs.

Seneviratne, M. and Cracknell, S. (1988) 'Consumer complaints in the public sector', *Public Administration*, 66(2): 181–93.

Severijnen, P. (1994) 'Local authorities and market research: market research incorporated in the policy process of consumer oriented local authorities'. *Local Government Studies*, 20(1): 34–43.

Skelcher, C. (1992) *Managing for service quality*. Managing Local Government series. Harlow: Longmans.

Smith, J. (1992) *Community development and tenant action*. Briefing Paper No. 2. London: Community Development Foundation and National Coalition of Neighbourhoods.

Smith, R., Gaster, L., Harrison, L., Martin, L., Means, R. and Thistlethwaite, P. (1993) *Working together for better community care*. SAUS Study. School for Advanced Urban Studies. Bristol: University of Bristol.

Social Services Inspectorate (1990) *Homes are for living in*. London: Department of Health, HMSO.

Solomos, J. and Back, L. (1993) 'Rethinking equal opportunities', in N. Thomas, N. Deakin and J. Doling (eds) *Learning from innovation: housing and social care in the 1990s*. Birmingham: Birmingham Academic Press.

Speller, S. (1992) *Service quality – the missing link? The need for a conceptual model*. Dissertation for MBA. Middlesex Business School (unpublished).

Speller, S. and Ghobadian, A. (1993) 'Excellence in local government: change for the public sector', in *Managing Service Quality*, September: 29–34. Bradford: MCB University Press.

Spencer, K. and Walsh, K. (1990) *Improving the quality of local authority housing management*. Birmingham: Institute of Local Government Studies, Birmingham University/Joseph Rowntree Memorial Trust.

Spray, W. (1992) 'The first estate management board in London', *Local Government Policy Making*, 19(2): 3–12.

Stewart, J. (1987) 'Has decentralisation failed?' *Local Government Policy Making*, 14(2): 49–53.

Stewart, J. (1994) 'Accountability and empowerment in the public services', in D. Gladstone (ed) *British social welfare: past, present and future*. London: UCL Press.

Stewart, J. and Walsh, K. (1989) *The search for quality*. Luton: Local Government Management Board.

Stewart, J. and Walsh, K. (1992) 'Change in the management of public services', *Public Administration*, 70(4): 499–518.

Taylor, M., Hoyes, L., Lart, R. and Means, R. (1992) *User empowerment in community care: unravelling the issues*. Studies in decentralisation and quasi-markets No. 11. Bristol: School for Advanced Urban Studies, University of Bristol.

Taylor, M., Langan, J. and Hoggett, P. (1994) *Encouraging diversity: voluntary and private organisations in community care*. Aldershot: Arena in association with Joseph Rowntree Foundation.

Taylor, P. (1991) *Consumer involvement in health care: synopsis of a review for the Swindon Health Authority* (duplicated leaflet). Devizes: Wiltshire and Bath Health Commission.

Thamesdown Evaluation Project (1993) *Enhancing practice through evaluation: opportunities for the voluntary sector.* Report by Joanne Moore and Gill Whitting, ECOTEC Research and Consulting Ltd. Birmingham: ECOTEC.

Waldegrave, William (1993) *Chancellor of the Duchy of Lancaster's speech to the Public Finance Foundation, 5 July 1993.* London: Office of Public Service and Science, Cabinet Office (transcript).

Walsh, K. (1991) 'Quality and the public services', *Public Administration,* 69(4): 503–14.

Walsh, K. (1993) 'Contracts', in N. Thomas, N. Deakin and J. Doling (eds) *Learning from innovation: housing and social care in the 1990s.* Birmingham: Birmingham Academic Press.

Walsh, K. and Davis, H. (1993) *Competition and service: the impact of the Local Government Act 1988.* London: Department of the Environment, HMSO.

Watkins, J., Drury, L. and Preddy, D. (1992) *From evolution to revolution: the pressures on professional life in the 1990s.* Bristol: University of Bristol in conjunction with the Clerical Medical Investment Group.

Webb, A. (1991). Co-ordination: a problem in public sector management, *Policy and Politics,* 19(4): 229–41.

Webster, B. (1990) 'Reviewing services for under-fives and their families in Gloucestershire', *Local Government Policy Making,* 17(3): 13–23.

Wener, R.E. (1985) 'The environmental quality of service encounters', in J. Czepiel *et al.* (eds), *The service encounter. Managing employee/customer interaction in service businesses.* Lexington, MA: Lexington Books.

Whittle, S. (1992) 'Total quality management: redundant approaches to culture change', *Quality of working: News and Abstracts,* 110, Spring: 8–13.

Williamson, C. (1992) *Whose standards? Consumer and professional standards in health care.* Buckingham: State of Health series, Open University Press.

Wills, J. (1991) 'Chartered streets', *Local Government Chronicle,* 17 May: 15–16.

Winkler, F. (1987) 'Consumerism in health care: beyond the supermarket model', *Policy and Politics,* 15(1): 1–8.

Wolverhampton City Council (1992) *Corporate complaints manual.* Handbook for staff training (unpublished).

Zeithaml, V., Berry, L.L. and Parasuraman, A. (1988) 'Communication and control processes in the delivery of service quality', *Journal of Marketing,* 52 (April): 35–48.

Index